FOREX
MADE EASY

FOREX
MADE EASY

6 Ways to Trade the Dollar

James Dicks

McGraw-Hill

New York   Chicago   San Francisco   Lisbon   London
Madrid   Mexico City   Milan   New Delhi
San Juan   Seoul   Singapore
Sydney   Toronto

5 6 7 8 9 0   DOC/DOC   0 9 8 7 6

ISBN 0-07-143894-7

This publication is designed to provide accurate and authoritative information in regard to the subject matter covered. It is sold with the understanding that neither the author nor the publisher is engaged in rendering legal, accounting, or other professional service. If legal advice or other expert assistance is required, the services of a competent professional person should be sought.

—From a Declaration of Principles jointly adopted by a Committee of the American Bar Association and a Committee of Publishers.

McGraw-Hill books are available at special quantity discounts to use as premiums and sales promotions, or for use in corporate training programs. For more information, please write to the Director of Special Sales, McGraw-Hill Professional, Two Penn Plaza, New York, NY 10121-2298. Or contact your local bookstore.

 This book is printed on recycled, acid-free paper containing a minimum of 50% recycled, de-inked fiber.

Library of Congress Cataloging-in-Publication Data

Dicks, James.
    Forex made easy : 6 ways to trade the dollar / by James Dicks.
        p.   cm.
    ISBN 0-07-143894-7 (Hardcover : alk. paper)
    1. Foreign exchange market.   I. Title.

  HG3851.D494 2004
  332.4'5—dc22   2003021906

THIS BOOK IS DEDICATED to my wife Deb. As I learned so well in the Marine Corps, there is no "I" in Team. It takes a team effort to make things happen. Deb is the team member that has been there through thick and thin. The long nights and the days away from home are hard. Deb has always had nothing but motivation, encouragement and love along the way, and with her love anything is possible. I love you dear.

Contents

Preface

WELCOME TO A NEW and exciting opportunity. It is called the foreign currency market (or the FOREX). My name is James Dicks, and I have been trading for more than 13 years. I have traded through many different market conditions and have seen first hand what such conditions can do to individual investors' portfolios.

I have spent most of my adult life and all of my younger years with my father and uncles as my mentors. My father is a very successful real estate investor, both commercially and residentially. My uncles, Jack and John, both attorneys and entrepreneurs, looked at me as their personal challenge in life, and I don't think I let them down.

Let me start from the beginning. I want to build a foundation so that you understand and know that I am no different than you are. Some of you may be older and wiser than I am, but I know one thing with which you cannot disagree: There is no reason for you to make the same mistakes I did, and if you have already made those same mistakes, I hope that you can learn from the solutions that I have found.

My family has always been one to think outside the box. We have very strong genes when it comes to the entrepreneur spirit. I grew up in the hotel business, as my father had several. As I got older, I began to think a little differently. Interestingly, everything I thought of was directly related to the financial industry.

I went to work for my uncles in the late 1980s, and I learned about personal finance and investing; it was soon after that I got my first securities license and became a stockbroker. I watched as my firm educated investors on alternative investments such as oil and gas limited partnerships—a great alternative to the stock market. As things frequently seem, it appeared to be greener on the other side.

The stock market took off, and most of the investors who invested in these limited partnerships were very unhappy that they were only making 8 percent on their money; they wanted all their money in the stock market, especially the technology sector. What do you think happened? You're right. The market went down like the *Titanic,* and so did investors' portfolios.

I was on a plane recently sitting next to a gentleman, and we were talking about investing. I was sharing with him my knowledge of the FOREX, and come to find out, he had invested in one of our limited partnerships. He told me how he could not have been happier that he did this. He told me that he would have been completely wiped out if he had not simply diversified his portfolio, not to mention that he was really quite happy to be getting his monthly check annualized out at 8 percent for the last 2 years.

My message—one of diversification and good money management—without a doubt can help you in your quest for financial freedom.

After years of being a stockbroker, I took a little time off, traded for myself, invested in real estate, opened a retail store, and just tried to do what everyone wants to do—become financially independent. I made some real good money with my retail stores. I opened a few and sold them, invested in some real estate, and decided that I had to accomplish one of the goals on my lifetime list, so I joined the Marine Corps, volunteered for infantry, went to Parris Islands—not exactly a time share location, either—and then on to my military occupational school.

Respect for the Marines Corps runs very deep in my blood. I think I was a born Marine. I love the Corp, and I definitely got a very good education on discipline, something all traders must have. After getting out of the Marine Corps, I continued my real estate investing, and I was still trading in the stock market, although it was starting to get a little harder than just buying a technology stock.

I ultimately bought about $20 million in real estate, with a very sizable amount in equity. I started living the good life but soon learned one lesson that applies to trading—money management, something I didn't know much about. I ultimately lost everything I had. I overleveraged my portfolio. One of the things you will learn in this book is how to avoid overleveraging your account, a strategy that you will need to learn as a FOREX trader. Well, back to square one again for me. The good news is I was able to avoid ever having to file for any type of bankruptcy. I simply faced adversity, and as the Marines taught me, I overcame and adapted.

After all that, I decided to go back to what I knew most—trading. I was working with my Uncle Jack again and got together with a software company that claimed to make trading as easy as 1-2-3, red light–green light. Now, all of sudden, there is all this software out there to simplify some of the more complicated ways to trade, and the software in the case of the red light–green light that I am sure some of you are familiar with was Wizetrade.

I became very good friends with the owners of the company and even went out teaching the software because I believed in it so much. The problem came when the market continued to go down. I was not happy trading the stock market. Too many scandals were happening. The news was becoming absolutely ridiculous, and the market makers were out of control.

It was hard enough to trade the market without all that going on. I finally got so frustrated that I stopped trading the market altogether. I still to this day use the stock market for diversification. While looking for an alternative to the stock market, a friend of mine told me about the FOREX, and I was interested.

It seemed that this market had all the benefits I was looking for. I could trade 24 hours a day, 6 days a week, with no commissions and no gaps up or down. So I started learning about it. Just after the Commodities and Futures Modernization Act was passed in October 2000, I worked on my first FOREX training in Vancouver, Canada. This was the beginning of 2001. It was real slow going, and I couldn't convince anyone to listen to me. Can you believe that this market is bigger in volume daily than all the markets of the world combined for 3 weeks, the same market that big banks, institutions, and corporations of the world used to diversify their portfolios?

Over the years, I had spoken to and taught tens of thousands of people all types of investing, and I was really getting tired of hearing horror stories about people's portfolios. The technology market was crashing, and people were losing upwards of 90 percent of their portfolios. Some stocks were going from $300 to $1. And all the while, investors were riding them all the way down. Worse yet, some investors were adding to their positions, cost averaging down.

In most cases such actions are all mistakes. You have to have a plan and trade the plan. You have to avoid trading emotionally, and you have to use diversification and good money management. You have heard, "Don't put all your eggs in one basket." Diversification doesn't mean that you should have your money spread out over a bunch of stocks. Or maybe several sectors. It means using multiple opportunities that spread your potential risk of loss.

In this book I have put together what I feel to be a very investor-friendly understanding of the FOREX and how to trade it. There are plenty of ways to make this more complicated, but there is no reason. This book is not for the investor who wishes to be an economist. This book is for the everyday investor who is looking for an alternative to the stock market for better portfolio diversification.

Acknowledgments

I FEEL LIKE I AM AT ONE of those big award shows and I just received an award. Now I have to make a quick speech and try to thank everyone that has been involved in this project without forgetting anyone. First and foremost I would like to just say thank you to my family. My wife Deb, my son James and my daughter Jacqueline. I am the luckiest man on the planet to have such a loving family.

My uncle Jack goes without saying. He has spent the last 14 years teaching me lesson after lesson. Some of those lessons I learned quickly and some not so quickly. Now my uncle Jack is also my partner and I have never had more fun working, than working with him. I also thank my Uncle John for his many years of that one little extra lesson. Thanks for taking the time to make sure I learned something and always believing in me. Thanks Mom for always being there for me and the love that you have given. I also thank my Dad for giving me the burning desire to succeed and all of the other family members that have helped me through the years. Can't forget the Marine Corps for teaching me never to quit and that anything is possible. Semper fi!

I give a special thanks to Mike Krajewski, Ari Paget, and Mike Stewart for all their help with this project. Couldn't have done it without you. Thanks guys!

Thank you all.

FOREX
MADE EASY

1

WHAT IS THE FOREX?

- Introduction
- FOREX Defined
- A Brief History of FOREX
- Free-Floating FOREX Market
- Major FOREX Participants

INTRODUCTION

There are more than 48 million household traders in the United States and more than 11 million are online with one purpose—to make profits from their investments and to take control of their retirement funds.

What is the purpose of investing? To make money, right! I have always said that the single greatest source for wealth is the stock market. It always has been and always will be. Well, this has been obscured somewhat over the last couple of years.

I have spent a great deal of time traveling across this great country of ours teaching people (investors) how to take control of their financial lives. I have spoken to many individual investors who have come up to me and told me their trading nightmares—told me that their portfolios have lost upwards of 90 percent of their value.

That in itself is a real tragedy, but what makes it worse is that many of these individual investors are approaching retirement; they do not have the luxury or the time to start rebuilding their retirement nest eggs. They are faced with some very harsh decisions. Well, let me tell you: It is never too late—you have to take action. If you don't, you will lose.

One of my favorite sayings is, "If you always do what you have always done, then you will always get what you have always gotten." Let's change this. I will teach you how you can start to make a difference just by increasing your awareness of and education about an alternative to the stock market, opening up opportunities that have long been available to *Fortune* 1000 companies, big banks, and institutions.

As a foundation to what I am going to be talking about, let's look at the biggest mistakes investors make, regardless of what market or what instrument they are trading.

MISTAKE 1: TRADE AGAINST THE TREND
This is the number one mistake that investors make today. They trade against the trend of their positions. Remember, "The trend is your friend."

Let's look at a perfect example of this: Do you remember the company whose stock prices are depicted in Figure 1-1?

Yes, it's Enron, and what has become known as the Enron debacle is a perfect example of investors trading against the trend. How about one of the biggest companies on Wall Street? Do you think that such a company would be a good investment for you portfolio? Probably so.

Look at Figure 1-1. Notice how the stock price is going down. The long-term trend on this is down—straight down. However, I want to point out a few things. First, there were a lot of Enron employees who loved the company. Most of the employees even took parts of their salaries as stocks and options.

Did you know that during the entire plunge of this stock, there was not one sell recommendation from a Wall Street analyst? Notice that as the stock went down from the $90 range, it had several *retracements;* that is, as the stock price was going down, it rallied and went back up a bit before going down again. As it was going down, what do you think investors were doing? They were buying. Why not—it was one of the biggest companies on Wall Street.

When the Enron stock price got to around the $65 mark, investors were somewhat relieved. They probably were saying, "Okay, it is now

FIGURE 1-1 Enron 2002–2003

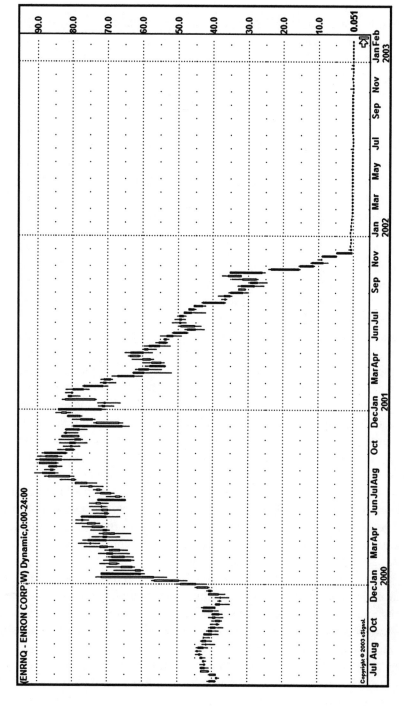

(ENRNQ - ENRON CORP;W) Dynamic,0:00-24:00

Copyright © 2003 eSignal.

finally going back up." Not so fast—the stock just retraced a little and started going back down again. Enron stock did this two more times, at $50 and $35, before falling off the map, so to speak. All the while, inventors were buying more.

MISTAKE 2: LISTING TO SO-CALLED EXPERTS

Look again at Figure 1-1. The entire way down, Enron stock had buy or hold recommendations from Wall Street analysts, never a sell. This is one reason why legislation was being discussed on Capitol Hill to solve this type of problem. The problem certainly was not limited to Enron. There was so much conflict of interest among analysts that most investors had a hard time keeping up with what was going on.

How many investors watch CNBC? Many, right? Well, where do you think the novice investors are getting their trading information? They get it from TV, newspapers, friends, and so on. The problem with this is that most of the information they are trading on is old, sometimes weeks old. You see this kind of thing happen all the time.

Let me give you an example. Let's say that ABC Company just announced that it has the greatest new computer in the world and that it will revolutionize the industry. What do you think is going to happen to the stock? It will go up, sometimes very quickly. However, usually the stock will turn around and go back down just as quickly when the volume dies down.

You see, in the world of stocks, there are market makers. These individuals have one objective in mind, and this is to make a fair and orderly market for a specific security. In the stock market, the reason a stock goes up is because there are more buyers than sellers, and the reason a stock goes down is because there are more sellers than buyers.

While the stock market is hard enough to trade with all the variables to keep in mind, the problem with the so-called experts is conflict of interest. The companies these experts work for are also market makers and own stocks. The opinions of these experts cannot be considered without considering their ulterior motives (see Figure 1-2).

Investor confidence is at an all-time low and has dropped dramatically as major investment firms are getting fined millions of dollars after recommending stocks to the public and yet at the same time sending internal memos and e-mails describing the lack of profit potential these same stocks actually had (see Figures 1-3 and 1-4).

I won't mention the firm I am referring to, but the improprieties continue. However, here is some good news. As I commented earlier, there

FIGURE 1-2   *James Dicks Buy Sell Hold*

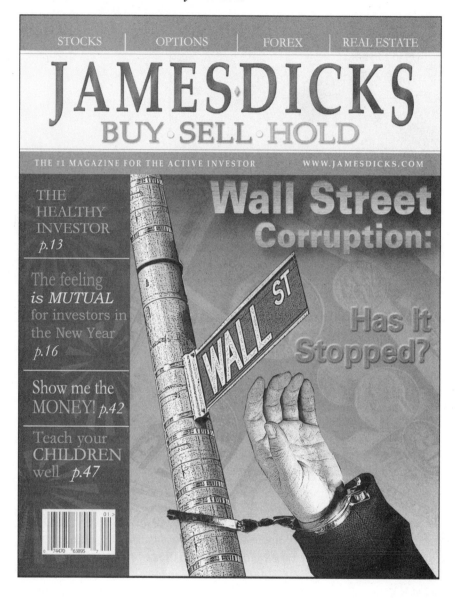

FIGURE 1-3 *James Dicks Buy Sell Hold*

is a lot of legislation being introduced, if not passed, on Capitol Hill to help clear up some of these problems.

The New York Stock Exchange (NYSE), as a self-regulating body, has taken on the task of changing the way it operates and has also taken the lead in cleaning up these problems. All the proposed and forthcoming changes will make a difference and ultimately allow for a better trading environment.

Next, there is a common falsehood among traders that for every buyer, there is a seller. This is not true. That is what the market makers are for. If there is not enough buying in a stock, then the market maker will come in and lower the price until there is more interest. The same holds true for selling. If there is not enough selling, then the market maker will start raising the price until there is more selling interest. This cycle repeats many times and is the basis of what is known as support and resistance. I will talk more about these concepts later.

MISTAKE 3: UNWILLINGNESS TO SELL
You have to be willing to cut your losers. There is no reason to ride a loser all the way down. You have to let your winners outpace your losers. You

FIGURE 1-4 *James Dicks Buy Sell Hold*

will learn a lot more about this when I get into good money management. I have heard investors tell me that they can't sell right now because they don't want to take a loss. "It is only a loss on paper." Okay, try spending it. It is a loss if you can't spend it, such as the Enron example. It never came back.

You would have been better off having a stop loss on your trade and having gotten out with a 25 percent loss to trade another day. I will cover stop losses as a way to use money management in your trading later. On the other hand, I have had investors say such things to me as, "If I sell it, I will have to pay taxes." Okay, if you have to pay taxes, why? Profit probably. As long as you have a plan for your taxes, don't be afraid to take your gains as well.

MISTAKE 4: EMOTIONALLY INVOLVED

This is my favorite. Let's look at Cisco Systems, a favorite story of mine to tell. I have personally experienced these changes in my portfolio, and my brother-in-law is a big salesman with the company.

The stock had split several times, and I bought some. It went back to $80, and I had dreams of retiring one day from trading this stock. A great many investors made millions on Cisco as it went to $80 and split several times, so surely I could do the same thing.

After hitting the $80 range in mid-2000, the trend reversed, and it was an excellent opportunity to short the stock if you had a crystal ball. However, I, like many individual investors out there, loved the company.

As the stock went down, I said to my self, "Hey, Cisco at $60. Wow, now that's a good buy." So guess what? I bought more. As it continued to go down, I started saying, "Well, it's got to go back up. It's a good company." It then dropped to $40. This is as low as it has been in a long time. The last time it was at $40, it went back to $80 several times (from the splits). This is the time to buy more.

Then Cisco went to $20. Now I again, like many other investors, said, "Wow! Well, I guess it is a good time to cost average down." This is what the professionals were saying. It had to be right. Then low and behold, the stock kept going lower, all the way down to about $11. Now here I am saying, "Well, I guess it can't go much lower." So I bought some more. Ultimately, it lost 85 percent from its high, and most investors bought more as it went down—buying into and adding to these positions. Why? Because of emotions.

Emotions and investing do not go hand and hand. Look at the Cisco chart for the time period I was referring to (Figure 1-5), and you will see how it had a few up trends (retracements). This is where all the investors were buying more.

Emotions—Here are a few things that I have said in the past while investing, and I am sure I was not alone:

"It will come back."

"It's a good company."

"It can't go any lower."

"I can't sell it now."

"I have a feeling about this one."

You might ask, then, "What can I do to invest wiser?" The answer is proper diversification. My grandmother told me so many times: "Don't put all your eggs in one basket." Guess what? I didn't listen until it was too late.

There is no difference with investing; your portfolio is your basket, so why would you invest all your money in the stock market or, worse yet, all in one sector of the market.

At my training classes, I have had investors come up to me and say, "I am diversified. I have my money in mutual funds." Sorry, that is still the stock market. Or, "I have my money in about 10 different tech stocks." Sorry, that is all one sector.

FIGURE 1-5 Cisco Weekly Chart 2002–2003

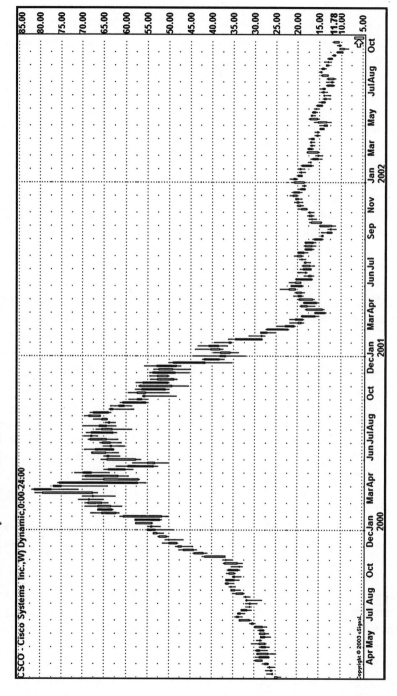

True diversification means just that. Put a portion of your portfolio in different areas, such as bonds, mutual funds, stock, real estate, options, annuities, and the FOREX. This is what the *Fortune* 1000 companies, big banks, and institutions do, so why don't you? Probably because *diversification* is a word that has been around for so long that we just forget what it means.

I like to say diversification is "common sense," just not "common knowledge." Well, it is now, because this is what I am going to teach you, as well as how to do it.

The foreign exchange market, FOREX for short, is the spot market for currency. Don't get this market confused with the futures market, where you buy a contract to purchase currency at a future price in time. The spot market does not have time value associated with it; therefore, there are no deltas, thetas, or intrinsic value to worry about. Don't stop reading, because it gets real easy. In fact, in my opinion, this market is easier to trade than the stock market. I will explain.

The spot foreign currency market is where traders come to trade the U.S. dollar. Have you ever heard of Bank of America? Certainly it is one of the largest, if not *the* largest, bank in the United States. Well, it uses the FOREX to diversify its portfolio, and so do numerous other banks.

If you go on the Internet, you can go to the Bank of America Web site and look under "Investor Relations." There you will find Bank of America's annual reports. This is public information and free. In the annual reports, which, by the way, are very long and detailed, you will find a category classified as "Global investment income" (see Figure 1-6).

On page 41 of the 2001 annual report (Figure 1-7) you will see where the Bank of America had $541 million in foreign exchange revenue, up $5 million.

If this market is good enough for the big banks, it's good enough for you. This market was made available to the average investor in 1998, and it is one of the fastest growing markets in the world.

With daily volume of nearly 100 times that of the stock market and available to almost anyone in the world, it is almost mandatory for you to invest in this market to properly diversify your portfolio.

The FOREX allows you to practice money management to its fullest, and because it is open 24 hours a day 6 days a week it doesn't see the same gap ups/downs, you never have to worry about your stop limit being skipped. Equally, the worry of companies posting false information and money managers or experts offering biased opinions will not have a large impact on a country's currency.

The FOREX trades currency pairs, which offers equal risk for short and long positions due to one of the currencies always having a bull

FIGURE 1-6   Bank of America 2001 Annual Report

Global Corporate and Investment Banking

Global Corporate and Investment Banking provides a broad array of financial services such as investment banking, capital markets, trade finance, treasury management, lending, leasing and financial advisory services to domestic and international corporations, financial institutions and government entities. Clients are supported through offices in 34 countries in four distinct geographic regions: U.S. and Canada; Asia; Europe, Middle East and Africa; and Latin America. Products and services provided include loan origination, merger and acquisition advisory, debt and equity underwriting and trading, cash management, derivatives, foreign exchange, leasing, leveraged finance, project finance, structured finance and trade services.

Global Corporate and Investment Banking
(Dollars in millions)

	2001	2000
Net interest income	$4,592	$3,725
Noninterest income	4,639	4,444
Total revenue	9,231	8,169
Provision for credit losses	1,275	751
Cash basis earnings	2,022	1,897
Shareholder value added	644	336
Cash basis efficiency ratio	54.3%	57.4%

→ In 2001, total revenue increased $1.1 billion, or 13 percent, primarily due to $620 million, or 22 percent, growth in trading-related revenue.

   → Net interest income increased $867 million, or 23 percent, as a result of higher trading-related activities and the Corporation's overall asset and liability management, partially offset by lower commercial loan levels.

FIGURE 1-7   Bank of America 2001 Annual Report

Trading-related revenue increased $620 million to $3.4 billion in 2001, due to a $543 million increase in the net interest margin and a $77 million increase in trading account profits. Increases in the fixed income, interest rate and commodities contract categories were partially offset by a decrease in equities and equity derivatives contracts. Fixed income showed the largest increase, up $483 million, or 129 percent, primarily attributable to an increase in market liquidity which resulted from a lower interest rate environment, as well as tightening of credit spreads. Revenue from interest rate contracts increased $198 million to $893 million reflecting a more volatile rate environment as well as an increase in customer flow as customers sought to lock in lower rates. Commodities contracts increased $102 million to $172 million, attributable to market volatility and increased customer flow. Foreign exchange revenue increased $5 million to $541 million. Income from equities and equity derivatives contracts decreased $168 million to $920 million, due to a slowdown in customer activity in the market. Trading account profits in 2001 included a $19 million transition adjustment gain resulting from the adoption of SFAS 133.

Trading-related Revenue in Global Corporate and Investment Banking
(Dollars in millions)

	2001	2000
Trading account profits	$1,818	$1,741
Net interest income	1,566	1,023
Total trading-related revenue	$3,384	$2,764
Trading-related revenue by product		
Foreign exchange contracts	$541	$536
Interest rate contracts	893	695
Fixed income	858	375
Equities and equity derivatives	920	1,088
Commodities	172	70
Total trading-related revenue	$3,384	$2,764

→ Investment banking income increased $67 million to $1.6 billion in 2001. Increases in securities underwriting and other investment banking income were offset by declines in syndications and advisory fees. Securities underwriting fees increased $177 million to $797 million from strong growth in high grade and high yield origination which was offset by lower equity underwriting. Syndication fees decreased $119 million to $402 million in 2001 as a result of fewer deals in the marketplace. A sluggish market for advisory services drove a decline in fees of $22 million to $276 million in 2001. Investment banking income by major activity follows:

side. For example, entering a long position on EUR/USD means that you are going long on the euro (EUR) and short on the U.S. dollar (USD), and it works the same way when you enter a short position on EUR/USD, in which you are actually going short on the euro and long on the U.S. dollar.

The FOREX has had a large impact on all the major banks, which are posting larger profits each year. Bank of America reported in its 2002 annual report a $530 million profit from foreign exchange revenue. Meanwhile, it reported only $384 million from equities and $86 million from commodities. The 2002 revenues grew to $530 million from only $5 million in 2000.

FOREX DEFINED

FOREX is the acronym for the *for*eign *ex*change market, where one country's currency is exchanged for that of another through a floating-exchange-rate system. It is the world's largest financial market, with an estimated daily average turnover of upwards of $2.5 trillion.

FOREX trading is not bound to any one trading floor and is not a market in the traditional sense because there is no central exchange. Instead, the entire market is run electronically, within a network of banks, continuously over a 24-hour period. The market opens Sunday at 5 P.M. (EST) and goes thru Friday afternoon at 4:30 P.M. (EST).

Banks have a natural flow of foreign exchange business from their customers, who buy and sell currency according to their individual needs. The banks must manage their own currency deposits in the changing light of their customers' transactions. To hedge or not to hedge? This is a way to basically minimize their potential for loss, often referred to as a *hedge*.

Investment managers also now deal globally, and they also must take positions in the different currencies, as well as in more traditional instruments, such as bonds and equities. For example, if a mutual fund is invested in U.S. bonds, the manager must decide if the fund should be invested in U.S. dollars or in a different currency. Again it is a question of hedging, another layer of risk to manage.

Conversely, because currencies have become an asset class, managers also must decide if the creation of a foreign currency exposure is desirable for speculative purposes. For example, it is possible to be long (to have bought) on the Nikkei Dow and short of (to have sold) the Japanese yen. In this case, the manager is using his or her knowledge of currency fluctuations to hedge in equity index position.

Companies and institutions of all kinds that have foreign customers or suppliers must decide if they should hedge the foreign exchange exposure that this creates. Exporters have the risk of a rise in the value of their local currency, and importers have the risk of a fall in theirs. If there is a change in currency value before the goods are exchanged, one of the parties could lose all their expected profits. This uncertainty in expected profits can be eliminated by offsetting the risk in the currency exchange.

As a result of these types of transactions, noninterbank turnover in the FOREX now accounts for about 25 percent of all transactions (21 percent in 1992).

A BRIEF HISTORY OF THE FOREX

In theory, foreign exchange dates back to ancient times, when traders first began exchanging coins from different countries and groups. However, the foreign exchange industry itself is the newest of the financial markets.

In the last hundred years, the foreign exchange market has undergone some dramatic transformations. In 1944, the postwar foreign exchange system was established as a result of a multination conference held at Bretton Woods, New Hampshire. That system remained intact until the early 1970s.

At this conference, representatives from 45 nations met together to discuss the future exchange system. The conference resulted in the formation of the International Monetary Fund (IMF). It also produced an agreement that fixed currencies in an exchange-rate system would tolerate 1 percent currency fluctuations to gold values, or to the U.S. dollar, which was established previously as the "gold standard." The system of connecting the currency's value to gold or the U.S. dollar was called *pegging*.

In 1971, the Bretton Woods Accord was first tested because of dramatically uncontrollable currency rate fluctuations. This started a chain reaction, and by 1973, the gold standard was abandoned by President Richard M. Nixon. The fixed-rate system collapsed under heavy market pressures, and currencies finally were allowed to float freely. Thereafter, the FOREX quickly established itself as *the* financial market, the world's largest financial market.

FREE-FLOATING FOREX MARKET

The foreign exchange markets officially switched to a free-floating market after the double demise of the Smithsonian Agreement and the European Joint Float. This switch occurred more due to lack of any other available options, but it is important to understand that the free floating of currency was not by any means imposed. This means that countries were free to peg, semipeg, or free-float their currencies.

FREE-FLOATING CURRENCIES

When the major currencies are free floating, such as the U.S. dollar, they move independently of other currencies. The value of the currency is determined by supply and demand, which has no specific intervention point that has to be observed, and can be traded by anybody so inclined. Free-floating currencies are in the heaviest trading demand.

SEMIPEGGED CURRENCIES

Semipegged currencies have disappeared since 1993. A perfect example of semipegging would be the currencies of the European Monetary System (EMS). Those currencies would be allowed to fluctuate only within 2.25 percent or, exceptionally, within 6 percent intervention bands. Following the foreign exchange crisis of 1993, the new EMS intervention rates were expanded to 15 percent. Semipegging would have a slowing-down effect on currencies when they were reaching the extreme values allowed within the range.

Since 1999, the semipegged currencies of the EMS were switched to fully pegged values that form the Euro.

PEGGED CURRENCIES

Some smaller economies have attached their currencies to larger economies with which they hold close economic liaisons. For instance, many Caribbean nations, such as Jamaica, have pegged their currencies to the U.S. dollar.

MAJOR FOREX PARTICIPANTS

Major FOREX participants include commercial and investment banks and central banks. Other participants include corporations, hedge funds, and millions of traders worldwide. The top seven banks that provide liquidity in this market include Bank of America, Credit Suisse, First Boston, Goldman Sachs, HSBC, J.P. Morgan, Morgan Stanley, Dean Whitter, and UBS Warburg.

As times change and many individual investors begin looking for an alternative to the stock market, the FOREX is growing every day, with average daily volumes reaching upwards from $1.5 trillion to $3.5 trillion. Now more than ever, the FOREX will play a key role in the wealth transfer of tomorrow.

2

MORE FOREX

- Currency Pairs
- Recommended Currency Pairs
- Why Trade the FOREX?
- Volume in the FOREX
- Analyzing the FOREX
- How Profits Are Made
- The FOREX as a Two-Way Market

CURRENCY PAIRS

Currencies are traded in pairs, for example, U.S. dollar/Japanese yen or U.S. dollar/Swiss franc. Every position involves the buying of one currency and the selling of another.

Have you traveled abroad? If so, then you are probably familiar with currency exchange rates. Most people living in the United States are not subjected to daily needs of currency exchange, but let's say that you decide to take a trip to Canada. As soon as you cross the border, you will start to find a need to exchange your U.S. dollars for Canadian dollars.

You will receive slightly more than 1.25 times your U.S. dollars in Canadian dollars. Not a bad day's worth of work. In fact, with the currency exchange rates, most people take extra cash and go shopping. Just don't have any left over when you return home because it will have the opposite effect on your wallet.

Let's look at another example. You are a chief executive officer (CEO) of a big international construction company. Your company specializes in building roads, and you just got a contract to build roads in Saudi Arabia. It is going to take about 5 years to build the roads, and you are going to be paid $20 million over the next 5 years. What do you do?

Do you take the job and start building the roads? No! The first thing you have to do is hedge the dollar value of your project. If it takes 5 years to complete your road-building project, there will be considerable fluctuation between the dollar and the reale, the local currency of Saudi Arabia.

What if there was a war or economic unrest in the area? Do you think that such an event can cause fluctuations in the currency exchange rates? If so, the thing to do is hedge. Most large corporations will hedge, which means they offset or opposite their position. In the case of building roads in Saudi Arabia, the CEO would buy or sell the U.S. dollar against the future value of the reale.

If the hedge is correct, then the road-building company will not lose any money if the reale goes up or down against the U.S. dollar over the 5 years. Multinational corporations and big banks do these types of investment every day, thus creating the daily tremendous volumes in the marketplace.

Take a look at some of the biggest banks mentioned in this book. Look at their annual financial statements, published every year and available to individual investors via their 10k's (annual reports). Most of these reports are listed on the banks' Web sites under "Investor Relations."

As you start to read through these very extensive reports, some hundreds of pages, you can see where these banks make all their money. Look for a heading that says, "Global Investment Income." When you do, you will see that millions and millions of dollars are made just on the exchange of currency.

RECOMMENDED CURRENCY PAIRS

While there are scores of currency pairs to choose from, the following currency pairs in Figure 2-1, due to their volume and liquidity in the market, are the most widely traded. It is important to keep in mind that you will be a much more successful trader if you concentrate on only a few currencies to trade rather than all the available ones.

Just like the stock market, when you start worrying about 40,000-plus stocks, it is hard to find the right currency pair to trade. Limit yourself and become an expert on just a few currencies you want to trade.

Currency that trades against the U.S. dollar is the most popular. It is the most liquid and volatile, which allows you as a trader to have a better opportunity to make a profit.

In addition to the currency pairs, there are also cross-currency pairs. Instead of trading against the U.S. dollar, one foreign currency trades against another non-U.S. currency, for example:

(EUR/CHF)

(CHF/JPY)

There are many different ones, but again, stay focused and concentrated on the U.S. cross-currency pairs.

As you may have noticed, currencies are displayed, for example, as EUR/USD. The base currency is the currency that is displayed in Figure 2-1. An easy way to remember which currency is the base currency is to look at how they are displayed.The currency in front, such as the EUR above, will be the one that is going up in value if the currency pair is going up, and if the currency pair is going down, then the EUR would be getting weaker.

FIGURE 2-1   Currency pairs.

Australian dollar	(AUD/USD)	Euro dollar	(EUR/USD)
British pound	(GBP/USD)	Japanese yen	(USD/JPY)
Canadian dollar	(USD/CAD)	Swiss franc	(USD/CHF)

FIGURE 2-2   Dollar Volume by Market

Year	NASDAQ	NYSE	AMEX
1980	$68,669,000,000	$374,909,300,000	$35,788,327,624
1981	$71,057,000,000	$389,218,600,000	$24,520,205,419
1982	$84,189,000,000	$488,395,300,000	$21,056,649,904
1983	$188,284,595,000	$765,275,200,000	$31,237,023,941
1984	$153,453,903,000	$764,737,800,000	$21,376,098,408
1985	$233,454,049,000	$970,478,700,000	$27,838,566,791
1986	$378,215,986,000	$1,374,349,600,000	$45,356,898,691
1987	$499,854,773,000	$1,873,597,200,000	$50,469,993,686
1988	$347,089,139,000	$1,356,049,600,000	$30,921,806,605
1989	$431,381,099,000	$1,542,845,000,000	$44,401,174,619
1990	$452,429,922,000	$1,325,332,400,000	$37,714,827,819
1991	$693,852,037,000	$1,520,164,000,000	$40,919,297,189
1992	$890,785,036,000	$1,745,466,400,000	$42,238,331,156
1993	$1,350,100,413,000	$2,283,369,600,000	$56,736,607,000
1994	$1,449,300,889,700	$2,454,241,600,000	$58,511,171,000
1995	$2,398,214,491,477	$3,082,915,308,000	$72,716,804,959
1996	$3,301,777,043,830	$4,063,654,600,000	$76,503,030,000
1997	$4,481,691,314,097	$5,777,601,500,000	$143,230,143,047
1998	$5,758,600,000,000	$7,287,948,500,000	$283,057,962,603
1999	$11,013,200,000,000	$8,945,195,000,000	$477,821,668,891
2000	$20,395,335,312,759	$11,060,046,000,000	$945,390,686,492
2001	$10,934,572,483,278	$10,489,322,500,000	$817,041,590,380

18

Thus, if the EUR/USD goes up in price, then the EUR is getting stronger against the dollar, and it takes more U.S. dollars to equal a euro. The same thing is true in reverse if the EUR/USD goes down. Whenever you have a currency pair that is at 1.00 even, then it is considered to be in *parity*. This is when one U.S. dollar would equal one euro.

WHY TRADE THE FOREX?

There are many benefits in trading the foreign exchange market (the FOREX). A few of them are

- It has continuous liquidity.

- It has very low dealing costs; 4 to 5 price interest point (pip; discussed later in this chapter) spreads.

- It has 100:1 leverage for margin trading.

- It has a very volatile, trending market.

- It has a two-way market; that is, traders participate in bull or bear markets.

- It is open 24 hours a day from Sunday night to Friday afternoon.

- There are no separate commissions.

VOLUME IN THE FOREX

The Central Bank Survey of Foreign Exchange and Derivatives Market Activity, coordinated by the Bank for International Settlements in March 1995 and published in May 1996, stated that turnover in the FOREX grew by 45 percent to $1.2 trillion between 1992 and 1995 (comparable figures for April 1989 and April 1992 were $590 billion and $820 billion, respectively).

The NASDAQ's dollar volume in 2001 reached $10.9 trillion, an increase of $10.2 trillion since 1991. This is a 1557 percent increase in the last 10 years (see Figures 2-2 and 2-3).

Official figures show the U.S. dollar on one side of 83 percent of spot foreign exchange transactions and in 95 percent of all deals in the swaps market. The euro remains the second most important currency in the foreign exchange market, with 37 percent (40 percent in 1992). The Japanese yen (24 percent) and the British pound sterling (10 percent) are ranked third and

FIGURE 2-3   Dollar Volume by Market

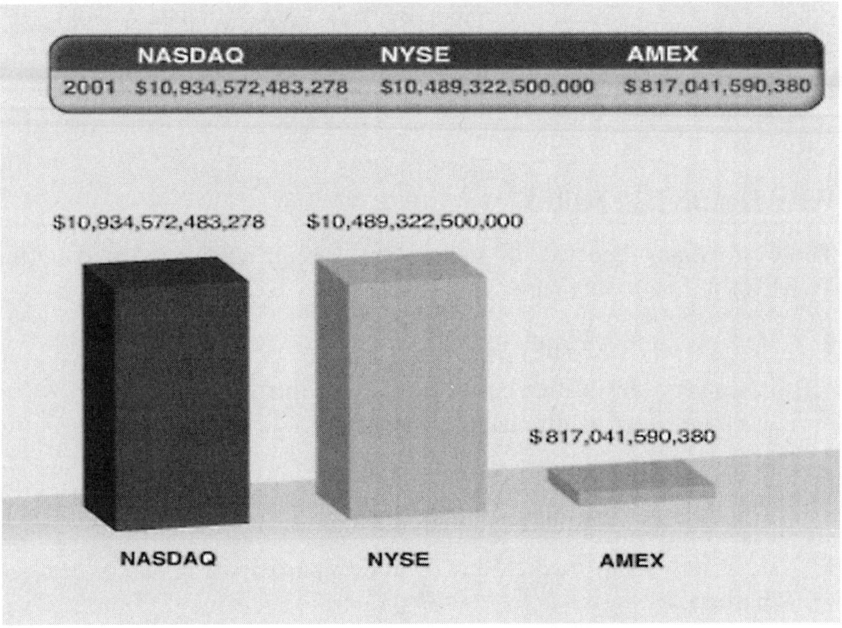

	NASDAQ	NYSE	AMEX
2001	$10,934,572,483,278	$10,489,322,500,000	$817,041,590,380

$10,934,572,483,278 $10,489,322,500,000

$817,041,590,380

NASDAQ   NYSE   AMEX

fourth. The Swiss franc's share was 7 percent, and both the Australian and Canadian dollars accounted for 3 percent. Perhaps the most interesting statistic is "Other Currencies," which now account for 8 percent and rising.

As a result of the consolidation of currencies with the development of the euro, nearly 90 percent of the daily volume in the FOREX passes through these six major currency cross rates even though the bulk of all exchange transpires through the United Kingdom, the United States, and Japan.

Unlike the stock market, where there are more than 40,000 stocks to choose from, a foreign currency trader needs to follow only the six major currencies and their relative pairings. To take this a step further, most of the professional currency traders around the world concentrate only on three currency pairs (see Figure 2-4). The EUR/USD and the USD/JPY are probably the two most heavily traded currency pairs.

LONDON: CAPITAL OF THE WORLD
London remains the world's largest foreign exchange center, with daily turnover during April 1995 of $464 billion (60 percent higher than the $290 billion recorded in April 1992), or 35 percent of the world's total daily volume.

FIGURE 2-4   Volume by Country 2001

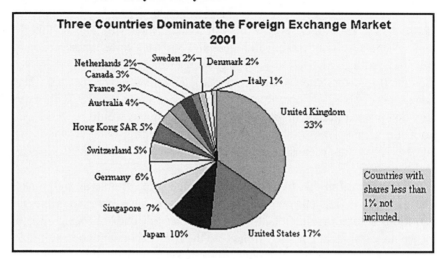

In the same period, both the Federal Reserve Bank of New York and the Bank of Japan reported smaller percentage increases of 46 and 34 percent, to $244 billion and $161 billion, respectively (compared with $167 and $120 billion in 1992).

The next four most important centers are Singapore, Hong Kong, Switzerland, and Germany, with daily turnovers ranging from $105 billion to $76 billion. France was ranked eighth, with a turnover of $58 billion.

In London, U.S. dollar/euro and U.S. dollar/Japanese yen trading account for 22 and 17 percent, respectively, of all transactions. Turnover in British pound sterling/U.S. dollar accounts for about 11 percent, and overall, the proportion of trades that involve British pounds sterling has fallen from 24 percent in 1992 to 16 percent at present.

A larger share of business in both the U.S. dollar (30 percent) and the euro (28 percent) takes place in London rather than in either the United States (16 percent) or Germany (10 percent). London is also the most important site, after its own domestic markets, for the trading of Japanese yen, Swiss francs, and Canadian and Australian dollars.

In addition, London remains the most diversified foreign exchange market. In New York, 64 percent is between the U.S. dollar and the four major currencies (euro, Japanese yen, British pounds sterling, and the Swiss franc; 74 percent in 1992), compared with 55 percent in London (59 percent in 1992). In Tokyo, the range of currencies traded is even more limited; the U.S. dollar/Japanese yen accounts for 76 percent of turnover, up from 67 percent in 1992.

While London remains the world's foreign exchange capital, the North American principals continue to be the most active, with a 42 percent market share. As you know, there is only one way to make money trading anything— buy lower and sell higher (or sell higher and buy back lower for short sales).

To buy lower and sell higher, prices must trend higher from where you bought (or lower from where you sold). If prices never trended, there would never be an opportunity to make a profit. Furthermore, without up and down price trends, institutional traders (hedgers) would have no need to insure themselves from price changes, and trading volume would disappear. What this means is that price trends are the essence of all profitable trading.

The realization that trends are the essence of profitable trading makes the idea of trading currencies very exciting because currencies are the world's best trending markets. Countless studies of trend-following systems prove invariably that currency trends are the most consistent and profitable.

Regardless of the type of trend-following system used—long term, intermediate term, or short term—currencies invariably outperform all other markets, including stocks, bonds, and other commodities. It should come as no surprise that some of the world's most successful traders are currency traders.

One reason that currencies trend better than every other market is because of their macroeconomic nature. Unlike many commodities whose supply and demand fundamentals literally can change with the weather, currency fundamentals are much less random and far more predictable.

For example, let's consider interest-rate differentials. Assume that U.S. interest rates are 4 percent and German interest rates are 6 percent. If you could borrow $1 million at 4 percent from one bank and invest it at 6 percent at another bank, would you? Of course you would! (With interbank currency trading, you can.)

The difference between 4 and 6 percent will attract international investors to borrow billions of U.S. dollars at 4 percent and invest them in German marks at 6 percent. Remember, such interest-rate differentials between countries are likely to last for some time. The United States would never change interest rates from 4 to 6 percent overnight, nor would Germany change interest rates from 6 to 4 percent overnight.

Large changes in interest rates over a short time could cause economic chaos. Therefore, as long as investors can buy German marks with U.S. dollars and receive sizable profits, billions of dollars will continue to buy those German marks, pushing prices for them ever higher (a classic trend). This is just one of several important reasons why currency trends tend to be so long and pronounced.

The FOREX has experienced spectacular growth in volume ever since currencies were allowed to float freely against each other. While the daily volume in 1977 was US$5 billion, it increased to US$600 billion in 1987 and reached the US$1.5 to 2.5 trillion mark since 2000.

In summary, currencies are one of the best all-around markets. Interbank currencies represent the world's largest marketplace and have the most powerful and persistent price trends. Propensities for strong and sustained price trends give interbank currency traders a profit-making edge that is unavailable in any other market.

ANALYZING THE FOREX

The forces of supply and demand determine the values of currencies. Speculation in the FOREX must be based on sound analytical principles. There are two radically different methods of forecasting where the forces of supply and demand are heading.

The first method, known as *fundamental analysis*, focuses on the actual events that are believed to have caused market movement in the past.

The second method, *technical analysis*, makes judgments based on the patterns and behavior of price data and indicators as they are displayed on charts.

There are several ways to trade the FOREX, such as charts and graphs and next-generation software. I found a piece of next-generation software called 4X Made Easy, which takes numerous different technical analyses and combines them with an algorithm that gives you buy and sell opportunities.

The important thing to note about this is that because the computer does the calculations for you, it does it the same way every time, with no deviations and no emotions. To be successful at trading, you must be able to duplicate success every time—trade the same way each and every trade.

Together with good money management, you only need to be right 50 percent of the time to make money. As long as your wins are greater than your losses, you can be a profitable trader. Good money management will bridge the gap.

HOW PROFITS ARE MADE

I make profits by using *margin* trading, where a relatively small deposit is required to control much larger positions in the market. My recommended brokers require a 1 percent margin deposit. Therefore, $1000 controls $100,000 of trade currency.

Currencies are traded in dollar amounts called *lots*. One lot is equal to $1000, which controls $100,000 in currency. This is margin. A *margin call* can occur when your trading account drops below this minimum $1000 per lot traded.

Currencies are traded on a *price interest point* (pip) system. Each currency pair has its own *pip* value. The goal of a trader is to capture as many profitable pips as possible. Values are determined by mathematical formulas and according to the exchange rate of the particular pair. Some pip values are fixed, whereas others can fluctuate slightly as one currency gains or loses strength against the other.

Below is a list of the six major currency pairs with their approximate price and pip values. The currency listed first in the pair is called the *base currency*. The current price of a currency is called the *spot rate*. (The fluctuating rates are subject to change over time.)

Currency	Approximate Price	Pip Value
Australian dollar (AUD/USD)	0.4920	$10.00 per pip (fixed)
Canadian dollar (USD/CAD)	1.5705	$6.80 per pip (fluctuating)
Swiss franc (USD/CHF)	1.7310	$7.20 per pip (fluctuating)
Euro (EUR/USD)	0.8810	$10.00 per pip (fixed)
British pound (GBP/USD)	1.4220	$10.00 per pip (fixed)
Japanese yen (USD/JPY)	123.50	$8.40 per pip (fluctuating)

PIP MOVEMENTS

As noted above, each currency price is a little different. For instance, the decimal point is placed differently for each currency. However, what remains the same is how we count pips for each currency from one *pip movement* to the next. The last digit in the currency price is where one pip moves to the next.

For example, in the Japanese yen (JPY), one pip movement higher is 123.50 to 123.51. For the euro (EUR), it is 1.0810 to 1.0811. For the British pound (GBP), it is 1.4220 to 1.4221. Therefore, a movement of 100 pips for the Japanese yen (JPY) is 123.50 to 124.50; for the euro (EUR), it is 1.0910 to 1.1010; and for the British pound (GBP), it is 1.4220 to 1.4320.

THE FOREX AS A TWO-WAY MARKET

In the FOREX, a trader can *enter* the market as a *buy position* (long) or a *sell position* (short). This is a tremendous advantage in the overall trading strategy. Since a trader can buy *or* sell when entering the market, it matters little if the currency he or she is trading is trending up or down.

Therefore, traders also can take advantage of strong up or down trends from their inception. This can be done because there are two sides to every currency cross-rate. Let's take a closer look at the euro (EUR) currency pair. The EUR is paired first with the U.S. dollar (USD). Since it is paired first, it is the *base* currency.

The FOREX cross-rate transaction involves the buying of one currency and the selling of the other. In this case, since the EUR is the base currency in this pair, we will be buying euros and selling U.S. dollars when we expect prices to rise. If we expect prices to fall, then we will *sell* euros and *buy* U.S. dollars.

The wonderful part about this intricate process is that it is nearly seamless through the broker software. The chart software and the broker software are in agreement with all sides of the currencies. Therefore, when we look at a chart and expect prices to rise, we *buy*. When we expect prices to fall, we *sell*.

When a trader believes that market prices will move higher, the trader will take a *buy position* in the market. As long as the trader sells back at a higher price, then he or she has captured profits. When a trader believes that prices will move lower, the trader will take a *sell position* in the market. As long as the trader buys back at a lower price, then he or she has captured profits.

Consider the screen shot and examples in Figure 2-5 that explain this trading process in detail.

In this example, a sell signal is indicated by arrow 1, identifying a selling position in British pounds at $1.5832 on July 26. After several days, we see a buy signal, and the short position is closed out by buying the British pound at $1.5211 on August 27. In this scenario, since the trader bought the British pound lower than he or she sold it, the trader would have made a profit of 521 pips.

The same holds true from the example entering in the opposite direction. Buying a position, meaning going long in British pounds, as indicated by arrow 2, results in a price of $1.5211 on August 27. After a few days, we see a sell signal, and the trader closes out the long position, indicated by

FIGURE 2-5 GBP/USD Daily Chart 2002–2003

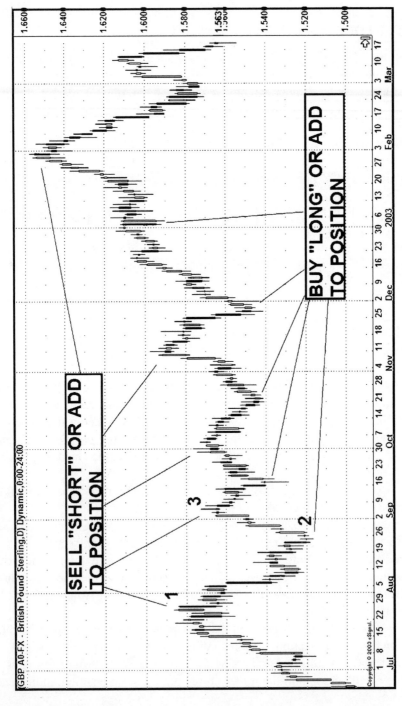

arrow 3. In this scenario, the price at the sell position is $1.5704 on September 6. This position could have made a 483-pip profit.

If a trader has entered a buy position and then must sell back at a *lower price* than the buy position, the trader takes a loss. If a trader who has entered a sell position and then must buy back at a *higher price* than the sell position, the trader takes a loss.

These examples are taken from real charts; however, these were only examples of how the market works in both directions. Using proper money management may have resulted in more or less profit.

3

FORECASTING
THE MARKET

- Fundamental Analysis
- Technical Analysis
- Fundamental versus Technical Analysis

FUNDAMENTAL ANALYSIS

The forces of supply and demand determine the value of currencies. Speculation in the foreign exchange market (the FOREX) must be based on sound analytical principles. There are two radically different methods of forecasting where the forces of supply and demand are heading.

The first method as mentioned earlier is known as *fundamental analysis.* While I cannot list all the events that move the market, some of them include the forces of currency supply and demand worldwide, fundamental economic data, and political developments.

Unlike in the stock market, fundamental analysis in the FOREX is much more important. Although it is important to watch fundamentals when trading in the stock market, it is much easier to manipulate the data. After all, where does the fundamental data come from that traders use to make their trading decisions?

Every publicly traded company has to produce 10q's and 10k's. These are their quarterly and annual reports, respectively. These reports have to be submitted to the Securities and Exchange Commission (SEC) on time and correct or the companies face fines and penalties. These reports have to go through the SEC for review before they are released to the general public of shareholders.

Does this ring any bells? How about the big problems of Enron, Global Crossing, and all the rest? If companies submit financial reports to the SEC that are not 100 percent accurate, how are you, the investor, supposed to know?

It is pretty hard, and this is exactly what happened at Enron. Investors were trading Enron stock thinking that it was one of the largest companies on the exchange, when, in fact, some of the fundamental data on the company were incorrect. In fact the company was much smaller than investors perceived.

In the FOREX, fundamental analysis has a much bigger emphasis. The fundamental data that I am talking about are usually key economic indicators. When these numbers are released, the various currencies will react.

If the numbers are different from expected, huge moves can take place. These huge moves can make or lose a trader a lot of money, depending on whether the trader is on the right side of the trade and/or the trader has used good money management.

This is an example of what traders look for in economic FOREX calendars (see Figure 3-1).

You can see that the forecast is what traders are building into the momentum of the currency. If the actual number comes in higher or lower than that predicted, the currency will react. These reports are used in all countries. The consumer price index (CPI) is calculated in all countries, some with different names but nonetheless the same type of measurement, and thus it would affect that country's currency.

When you are trading, be sure to know when the news is coming out. Ultimately, the trend in the currency will prevail, but unexpected news can affect the trend even if only for a very short time. The effect, however, can be enough to stop you out of your trade.

Don't worry, though; you do not have to know about these forecasts if you don't want to because there are numerous FOREX alert services out there. These alert services usually charge a monthly fee and will keep you apprised of news and what is anticipated, as well as what to expect if something unanticipated happens.

FIGURE 3-1 Schedule in the FOREX Market

THE WEEK AHEAD SCHEDULE IN FOREIGN EXCHANGE

Weekly Report

Events for week of 05/12/2003

Date	Time (EST)	Location	Description
5/16/2003	9:45:00 AM	US	May University of Michigan prelim
5/16/2003	8:30:00 AM	US	April CPI
5/16/2003	8:30:00 AM	US	April Core CPI
5/16/2003	8:30:00 AM	US	April Housing Starts
5/16/2003	6:00:00 AM	6:00 AM	April HICP y/y
5/16/2003	6:00:00 AM	E-12	April HICP m/m
5/16/2003	6:00:00 AM	E-12	April HICP m/m ex Food & Energy
5/16/2003	6:00:00 AM	E-12	April HICP y/y ex Food & Energy

I wanted something very specific, so I founded PremiereTradefx, a company that FOREX traders can use to open a demo trading account or a brokerage account to trade the FOREX. In addition, I have created FOREX Alerts, a software/service for which you can get a preview trial at *www.premieretrade.com*. My professional traders make trades and alert you to those opportunities as well as provide daily and weekly updates, and they will keep you informed of upcoming world and economic news.

TECHNICAL ANALYSIS

The second method is *technical analysis*. This is one of the oldest tools with which to trade. Technical analysis has been around for roughly 30 years. There are more than 150 different types of technical analyses that a trader can use. It is really up to the trader.

The common description of technical analysis is that you take past performance of a position, equity, currency, future, or whatever and tie it together with mathematical calculations to try to predict the future outcome of the position.

Technical analysis is based on three assumptions:

1. All available information and its impact on traders and the market are already reflected in a currency's price.
2. Prices move in trends or patterns.
3. History repeats itself.

These assumptions lead to the following conclusions:

- As a direct consequence of the first assumption, technicians believe that there is little to be gained by researching economic fundamentals.

- Technicians believe that fundamental research will lead to an explanation of the current price rather than an accurate forecast of future price.

- Fundamental analysts can only follow a limited number of aspects at one time.

- Price activity reflects most of the relevant fundamental events and their impact on most traders most of the time, so a technician enjoys a more complete perspective of all the activity unfolding than a "fundamentalist."

- The power of technical analysis is that it can be applied effectively to virtually any market.

Because of these overwhelming factors, I encourage technical trading rather than trading on fundamental analysis alone, but *not* traditional technical analysis. With the advancements in computer technology, we are now able to analyze the market technically using computer programming to measure supply and demand as well as many other factors, therefore eliminating the emotional and human discretionary aspects of trading.

There is so much interpretation when using technical analysis that traders looking at the same thing may see different things altogether. This is one reason that you will want to find a trader who is willing to share his or her perspective. Whether you use managed accounts or alerts or a mentor or a coach, it is imperative to your success as a trader to get as much training as you can to increase your potential for success.

Recent history in the stock market only proves my point. When stocks were going down—and I mean way down—many individual traders were buying more—that's right, more stock—even though the trends in both the stock and general markets were going down.

Investors were saying such things as, "It can't go any lower," "It is a good company," "It will come back," and so on." How about, "It's a good time to cost average down," "I can't sell it right now," and "It is only a loss on paper"? These are all things that have contributed to the demise of most traders' portfolios—simply because they failed to follow the basic trend reversals.

FUNDAMENTAL VERSUS TECHNICAL ANALYSIS

A "fundamentalist" studies the cause of market movement, whereas a technician studies the effect. Most traders would classify themselves as both technicians and fundamentalists. In reality, there is a lot of overlap in information and how each factor ends up moving the market one way or another.

Most fundamentalists will have knowledge of charts, indicators, and chart analysis. Similarly, most technicians will have knowledge and awareness of the fundamentals. The problem is that the charts and fundamentals are often in conflict with each other, because one tries to predict the future with present events and the other uses history to predict the future.

I myself have always been a technician. I think that some of the mathematical calculations are extremely good at showing you where a potential trade can go in the future. Although technical analysis cannot predict the future, it can give valuable insight into where a trade is going.

As I will begin to tie all the strategies together in this book, you can see how the next-generation software that is out there can help investors of all types with an easier approach to investing. With more than 150 different types of technical analyses, it is hard to determine which one is right for you. I cover some of my favorites.

In the end, the approach to trading that is best for you is the one that feels the most comfortable and the one that you feel you can duplicate the best. To be successful in trading, you have to be able to duplicate your success every time.

CURRENCY OPTIONS

- Currency Options Introduction
- Option Pricing
- Advantages of Trading Options
- European and American Options
- Exotic Options
- Lock in Profits
- Accelerate Your Profits

CURRENCY OPTIONS INTRODUCTION

Options are used within many companies as a risk-management tool and are important in that process. Risk managers must have a good understanding of currency options as they apply to their unique position in the marketplace.

What is an option? Simply stated, an option is a choice. The buyer of an option acquires the right but *not* the obligation to buy or sell an underlying asset under specific conditions in exchange for the payment of a premium. It is entirely up to the buyer whether or not to exercise that right; only the seller of the option is obligated to perform.

In every foreign exchange transaction, one currency is purchased and another currency is sold. Consequently, every currency option is both a call and a put. A *call* option conveys the right to buy the underlying asset, and a *put* option gives the buyer the right to sell.

An option to buy Australian dollars against U.S. dollars is both an Australian dollar call and a U.S. dollar put. Conversely, an option to sell Australian dollars against U.S. dollars is an Australian dollar put and U.S. dollar call.

Let's take the example of an Australian importer who has the obligation in 3 months' time to pay US$1 million for a commodity such as soymilk. The importer has a number of alternatives:

- Remain unhedged and purchase the U.S. dollars at the prevailing spot rate in 3 months' time

- Hedge by buying U.S. dollars forward

- Hedge by using an options strategy

One of the many strategies available to an importer is to buy an Australian dollar put/U.S. dollar call option. The effect of buying an Australian dollar put is to place a ceiling on the cost of imports without limiting the potential benefit if the spot rate rises. The importer limits the cost to a maximum while not limiting the minimum.

OPTION PRICING

The premium quoted for a particular option at a particular time represents a consensus of the option's current value, which consists of two elements: intrinsic value and time value. *Intrinsic value* is simply the difference between the spot price and the strike price. A put option will have intrinsic value only when the spot price is below the strike price. A call option will have intrinsic value only when the spot price is above the strike price. Options that have intrinsic value are said to be "in the money."

Time value is more complex. When the price of a call or put option is greater than its intrinsic value, this is so because the option has *time value*. Time value is determined by five variables: the spot or underlying price, the expected volatility of the underlying currency, the exercise price, the time to expiration, and the difference in the "risk free" rate of interest that can be earned by the two currencies. Time value falls toward zero as the expiration date approaches.

An option is said to be "out of the money" if its price consists only of time value. A number of complex option pricing models such as the Black-

Scholes and Cox-Rubinstein models have been developed to determine option pricing. Another commonly used model for currency option valuation is the Garmen-Kohlhagen model.

Many texts cover the specifics of option pricing models in detail. Interest-rate differentials between nations and temporary supply/demand imbalances also can have an effect on option premiums. In the final analysis, however, option prices (premiums) must be low enough to induce potential buyers to buy and high enough to induce potential option writers to sell.

ADVANTAGES OF TRADING OPTIONS

Options offer a low-cost method of hedging or speculative spot trading with the ability to minimize risk for potentially high profit returns. The amount of capital risk is always known in advance. With the ability to fully customize your options, including payout amounts, barrier prices, and expiration dates, options have greater flexibility for different styles of trading.

EUROPEAN AND AMERICAN OPTIONS

The two parties to a currency option contract are the option buyer and the option seller/writer. The option buyer may, for an agreed-on price called the *premium,* purchase from the option writer a commitment that the option writer will sell (or purchase) a specified amount of a foreign currency on demand.

The option extends only until the expiration date. The rate at which one currency can be purchased or sold is one of the terms of the option and is called the *exercise price* or *strike price.* The details described in a currency option include the underlying currencies, the contract size, the expiration date, the exercise price, and another important detail—whether the option is an option to purchase the underlying currency—a *call*—or an option to sell the underlying currency—a *put.*

There are two types of option expirations—American-style and European-style. *American-style* options can be exercised on any business day prior to the expiration date. *European-style* options can be exercised at expiration only.

Currency options may be quoted in one of two ways—*American terms,* in which a currency is quoted in terms of the U.S. dollar per unit of foreign currency, and *European terms* (*inverse terms*), in which the dollar is quoted in terms of units of foreign currency per dollar. The same logic can be applied to currency pairs in which the U.S. dollar is not one of the currencies. Either currency can be expressed in terms of the other.

EXOTIC OPTIONS

There are five *exotic options* that are most popular:

1. Digital
2. No-touch
3. One-touch
4. Double no-touch
5. Double-touch

DIGITAL

Digital options are simple and inexpensive. If you believe that the EUR/USD will be above 1.0700 at the end of 2 months, but you are not exactly sure when this decline will occur, a digital option is perfect for you. You would simply buy a 2-month EUR call/USD put digital option with a 1.0700 strike. If after 2 months the EUR/USD rate is equal to or greater than 1.0700 at expiration, you would automatically earn your predetermined payoff. If not, your option simply would expire worthless. With low option premiums, your predetermined return can be in excess of 100 percent (see Figure 4-1).

ONE-TOUCH OPTIONS

This type of option is perfect for traders who anticipate a retracement and believe that the price of a given currency will test a support/resistance level. The one-touch option pays a fixed amount if the market touches the predetermined barrier level.

All you need to do is to determine the desired payoff, the currency pair, the barrier price, and the expiration date. As long as the spot level hits the barrier level at least once prior to expiration, you receive the payoff amount. If the barrier is not reached during the option period, the option expires worthless. The payoffs of the options are credited to the clients' account as soon as the market touches the barrier level.

NO-TOUCH OPTIONS

A no-touch option is a great way to profit from a trending market. The no-touch option pays a fixed amount if the market never touches the barrier level that you choose.

FIGURE 4-1   Good market calls, bad market timing

You trade 15-minute movements but also have a 2-month view.

EUR/USD now: 1.0300
I think: EUR/USD will be above 1.0700 in 2 months

Sample option: Buy 2-month EUR call/USD put digital option with $5000 payoff for $800.
Two months from now:

EUR/USD > 1.0700 = earn $5000 (minus the premium paid)
EUR/USD < 1.0700 = option expires worthless, lose $800

All you need to do is to determine the desired payoff, the currency pair, the barrier price, and the expiration date. As long as the spot level never hits the barrier price before expiration, you receive the payoff amount. If the barrier is reached during the option period, the option expires worthless.

DOUBLE NO-TOUCH

If you have a successful track record of identifying and profiting from breakouts but always lose money or do not make money in range markets, a double no-touch option is perfect for you. Breakouts are simply a currency pair such as the EUR/USD that has been trading around the same price for instance maybe it is 1.12-1.13. If the currency pair goes above the 1.13 or below the 1.12 it has now broken out of that range. That example wll also work as a range bound example. Lets say that the same EUR/USD is trading between 1.12 and 1.13. If the currency pair stays within that range of 1.12-1.13 it s range bound. Now lets look at a example of a double no-touch option;. If you are waiting for breakout levels in AUD/USD at 0.5400 or 0.5800 and expect this to happen within the next month, you can profit from the range trading market by buying a low-cost double no-touch AUD/USD option with 0.5400 and 0.5800 barrier levels and a payoff of $20,000 for $7000. In this way, if the AUD/USD does not break out within the next month, you will still earn $20,000. If it does break out, you will lose the $7000 premium paid for the option, but you will earn from your breakout strategy (see Figure 4-2).

DOUBLE ONE-TOUCH

If you are successful at picking tops and bottoms in a range market but can't sustain your losses in a breakout market, then a double one-touch option is perfect for you. For example, if you are range trading NZD/USD

FIGURE 4-2 Double no-touch option strategy

Breakouts, but you can't make money in range markets (to hedge against range markets).

AUD/USD now: 0.5600

I think: AUD/USD will break out of 0.5400 or 0.5800 in the next
    month, and I will make $20,000 in a breakout scenario

Sample option to hedge against no profits in range market: Buy 1-month AUD/USD double no-touch option with 0.5400 and 0.5800 barrier levels and a $20,000 payoff for $7000.

One month from now:

AUD/USD does not break out and does not touch 0.5400 *or* 0.5800
    = earn $20,000 (minus the premium paid)

AUD/USD breaks out and touches either 0.5400 or 0.5800 =
    option expires worthless, lose premium of $7000, but make
    expected breakout profits of $20,000

---

between 0.5100 and 0.5400 with good success but know that it may break 0.5100 or 0.5400 within the next 3 months, your losses could large. However, you can profit or reduce losses from a breakout by buying a double one-touch NZD/USD option with 0.5100 and 0.5400 barrier levels and a payoff of $15,000 for $1800.

In this way, if NZD/USD breaks out of those levels within the next 3 months, you will receive a payoff and reduce losses by $13,200. If it does not break out, you will lose the $1800 premium paid for the option, but you will earn from your range-trading strategy (see Figure 4-3).

LOCK IN PROFITS

If your option appreciates significantly in value, you can improve your option-trading returns by locking in profits. This is a very simple process; you simply sell the current option, and purchase a cheaper option with a different strike price or maturity.

By purchasing the cheaper option, you would be putting less money at risk, or taking profits. In addition, you would still be able to earn from further option appreciation if the currency market rate continues to move in your favor.

FIGURE 4-3   Double one-touch option strategy

You are great at picking tops and bottoms in a range market, but as soon as there is a breakout, you lose money (to hedge against breakout markets). Range trading works great for you, but market volatility or excessive movements are your pitfalls (to hedge against breakout markets)

NZD/USD now: 0.5250

I think: NZD/USD will range trade at 0.5100 or 0.5400 in the next 3 months, and I will make $8000

Sample option to hedge against losses: If NZD/USD breaks out of range, buy 3-month NZD/USD double one-touch option with 0.5100 and 0.5400 barrier levels and a $15,000 payoff for $1800.

Three months from now:

NZD/USD breaks out and touches either 0.5100 or 0.5400 = earn $15,000 (minus the premium paid)

NZD/USD continues to range trade and does not touch either 0.5100 or 0.5400 = option expires worthless, lose $1800, but make expected breakout profits of $8000

For example, suppose that you bought a 3-month EUR call/USD put option with a 1.0000 strike price when the current EUR/USD market rate was 0.9900. Now, EUR/USD is 1.0500, and you have made significant profits. You still believe that the EUR/USD will appreciate, but you want to lock in some profits.

What you do is to sell your original option and purchase a cheaper option, such as a 3-month EUR call/USD put with a 1.0300 strike price. The difference between what you earned when selling the original option and the new option premium is the amount of profits that you have "locked in." Given that you still own a EUR call/USD put option, you will continue to benefit from further EUR/USD appreciation.

ACCELERATE YOUR PROFITS

If you have a strong belief in the continued appreciation of your option value, you can increase your option-trading returns by accelerating your profits. This is also a very simple process. All you need to do is to sell your current option and use the funds to purchase cheaper options.

This would allow you to buy more of the cheaper options than you originally owned. This strategy is different from the strategy for locking in profits discussed earlier but is also useful.

For example, suppose that you purchased five lots of 1-month EUR call/USD put options with a 1.0200 strike price when the EUR/USD market rate was 1.0100 for $3350. Now, EUR/USD is at 1.0400, and your option is valued at $11,690. You still believe that the EUR/USD will appreciate, and you want to generate higher returns in a shorter period of time.

What you can do is sell your original option and purchase a cheaper option, such as a 1-month EUR call/USD put with a 1.0300 strike price. With the funds generated from your option sale, you potentially could purchase seven lots of the cheaper option. If the EUR/USD rate appreciated to 1.0500, the value of your new seven-lot 1.0300 strike option would be $16,425, whereas the value of the five lots of your original option at 1.0500 would only be $15,670.

Don't panic if you think what you just read is confusing. It is. You will find one option strategy that will work for you and then become good at it. Each strategy is designed for a very specific situation. This is why you need to concentrate on one strategy first. Learn that strategy, and then you can use it when the time is right.

If you find the option strategies easy to understand, then you may want to spend more time trading options rather than currency pairs. Just like the stock market, traders can become professionals at trading only options. The choice is yours.

5

CREATING A WORKSTATION FOR TRADING

- Workstation Location
- Trading Computer and Accessories
- Internet Connection
- Trading Software Programs
- Continuing Education

BEFORE WE GET TOO far into the nuts and bolts of analyzing market data and trading, we first must consider a very important factor in profitable trading. At first glance it may not appear that important, but you will come to appreciate the wisdom of ensuring that you have all the tools necessary to make your trading experience a positive one.

WORKSTATION LOCATION

Choosing the right place for trading is your first step. Be sure not to rush into making this decision too quickly. Do you have a spare room? How about an existing den or office?

The place you choose should be a place where there are few distractions—where you can concentrate and feel comfortable. Trading can be very stressful at times, so your trading area should be a place where you can relax. Avoid setting up your trading computer in your bedroom because this could disrupt your sleep cycle.

Having the right amount of rest and sleep is as important as learning the trading method itself. Try not to fall into an addictive approach to trading where all you want to do is trade 24 hours a day. Remember, this is not a sprint but a marathon. If there is nothing to trade, then don't trade.

You also may want to consider accessibility to a television at your workstation; if you have cable, this is even better. A lot of traders, including myself, have CNBC or CNBCW on while trading.

Unlike other financial markets, the foreign exchange market (the FOREX) is driven by real-time news. You will see the FOREX move before your eyes as news is released, especially prior to the commodities market opening at 8:30 A.M. (EST).

Being alerted to breaking news events will quickly cover the cost of adding cable or satellite television to your workstation, and of course, it is tax deductible under Internal Revenue Service (IRS) guidelines. I cover more of this in Chapter 15, "The Business of Trading."

TRADING COMPUTER AND ACCESSORIES

One of the most frustrating situations for a new trader is attempting to trade with outdated computer equipment. The following list of requirements must not be ignored in acquiring adequate computer equipment, especially if you are trading with next-generation software, some of which requires specific types of connections and processing speed. Refer to the box the software came in for the requirements.

Minimum hardware requirements include

- A Pentium II or greater with a 300-MHz processor

- 128 MB of RAM

- A 6-GB hard drive

- A 17-inch monitor or larger (some traders choose to connect two or more monitors)

- A 56-KBd modem (broadband recommended)

- A color printer

Whether you chose a desktop or laptop computer, be sure that it meets the minimum requirements for the best operating results. You also will want to have a comfortable chair with adequate lower-back support. You are going to be spending lots of stressful time in that chair, so get a good one, and you will thank yourself later.

There are numerous trading styles to choose from—long term, short term, active, day trading, swing trade, position, and custom trading. Any one of these can be right for you. You may find that you only trade once a week.

Other useful accessories include a small calculator, a telephone with autodial features to reach your broker fast if you have an online problem, a white board with dry-erase pens, and a notebook to be used as a trading log.

The trading log is helpful daily, but if you make good notes about your trades, you will soon discover *patterns to success*. The more you learn your own success pattern, the larger your profits will be. Every trader is a little different, and you want to know what *you* do best.

INTERNET CONNECTION

Along with an adequate computer, you also will need a stable Internet service provider (ISP). Avoid free Internet services because frequent disconnections are their norm. Dial-up services can range from $5 to $20 per month. Make sure that you sign up with an ISP that has more than one dial-up phone number as well as good customer support services.

Recently, Digital Subscriber Line (DSL) and cable services have become very popular. Neither DSL nor cable is required to run any of the trading software programs, but one or the other is recommended for several reasons. With a dial-up service, you risk a greater chance of being disconnected and much slower download speeds.

For those road warriors out there, I have even traded online using my cell phone or modem card. A warning: They are a much slower, and I do not recommend trading with them short term because the data streaming in may be delayed as a result of the slow connection speed.

INTERNET BROWSER

An Internet browser, either Internet Explorer 5.0 or higher or Netscape 6.0 or higher with Outlook, is required to view information on the numerous Web sites out there.

TRADING SOFTWARE PROGRAMS

There are several applications or software programs that can help you trade successfully. A few of the applications to consider are as follows.

DEALING STATIONS

In order to make trades in the FOREX, you will need a trading platform. It is through a broker that you will execute buy and sell orders that will become your trades. In the recent past, buying and selling currency only occurred over the phone and required verbal confirmation from both parties—the trader and the broker.

Because of advances in technology, currency buying and selling now can occur in seconds with a few clicks of the mouse—through a software interface between trader and broker. This software interface is called a *dealing station.*

Of course, the firm I recommend to trade with is the firm that I founded and designed from the bottom up to give traders the best tools. PremiereTrade as an introducing broker thru numerous market makers offers FOREX traders the highest level of price transparency via real-time streaming quotes and a speed of execution that is unmatched in the marketplace. There are other firms out there, though, and ultimately, the choice is yours. You can go to *www.premieretrade.com* for more information.

So how do brokers make money? They provide liquidity, act as the counterparts on their clients' transactions, and assume risk. In return, they attempt to earn a portion of the difference between the bid and offer (the dealing spread) instead of charging commissions.

FOREX electronic communications networks (ECNs) and trading firms without market-making desks are basically brokers who must charge commissions to earn revenue. Yet they offer the same 3- to 5-pip dealing spreads to their customers. So why pay a brokerage if you don't have to?

REAL-TIME EXCHANGE RATES

Bid and ask quotations are displayed continuously by the Internet Currency Trading System on a 24-hour basis for each currency pair. The quotations are updated thousands of times per day to reflect in real time the price at which a client can buy or sell any given currency pair.

EXECUTABLE QUOTATIONS

The prices displayed on the dealing stations are not indications of where the market is trading but actual prices at which the broker is offering to buy or sell. With two clicks of the mouse, clients can execute a trade at a displayed quotation.

There are several systems on the market that make a distinction between indicative quotations and executable prices. Although such systems show prices, the client must request a quotation to find out at what exchange rate a trade actually can be executed.

EXECUTE ORDERS BY PHONE

Clients may trade over the telephone with most brokers. The trading desks are usually in operation 24 hours a day from Sunday at 5 P.M. (EST) through Friday at 4:30 P.M. (EST).

When trading by phone, dealers will quote the same tight spreads available by dealing platform. All trades executed by phone are subject to a pre-deal margin availability check and will be entered manually into the customer's account for integrated profit and loss (P&L) analysis and reporting. All telephone calls are recorded for the safety of both parties.

SOFTWARE AND DATA FEED FROM eSIGNAL

With Version 7.0, eSignal began a process of turning the standard set of basic studies that were offered traditionally as part of the eSignal software package into a set that has a more robust user interface featuring customizable scaling, a wide array of user-friendly drawing tools, and the ability to accommodate user-defined studies.

The advanced charting versions of the line, bar, and candle charts were the logical choice for this "starter set" because of the very nature of their charting function—to make graphic representations of market activity—in other words, to create pictures from the numbers.

Figure 5-1 presents a sample of the quality charts that eSignal offers, and it is the software I chose for demonstrational charts for this book. I know the people at eSignal out in California, and they make a great product. They are very interested in seeing that all their clients are successful investors.

PREMIERETRADE AI

PremiereTrade AI is a powerful charting and instant trend analysis tool that receives real-time stocks, mutual funds, options and foreign currency price data and updates directly over the Internet. PremiereTrade AI boasts a winning combination of high-quality graphics matched with a complete set of money management analysis functions for almost any trade style.

FIGURE 5-1   GBP/USD Daily Minute Chart 2003

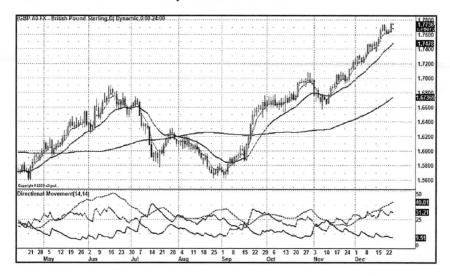

PremiereTrade AI's on-screen next-generation tools and technical analyses to confirm buying and selling opportunities for trader of all experience and background.

PremiereTrade AI is perfect for the novice or master trader. PremiereTrade AI provides real-time tracking and analysis of the top currencies in the world without the use of complex charts and graphs. Instead, its unique and simple green arrow, red arrow color indicator system identifies trends as well as possible entry and exit points.

This is the software that I founded. It was a dream of mine to have something that could allow individual investors easy access and trade ability to the FOREX (see Figures 5-2, 5-3, 5-4).

CONTINUING EDUCATION

World-class traders are always continuing their trading education. As you master the trading methods in this book, you will want to continue to educate yourself in FOREX trading.

I offer continuous online training as well as my national radio show, live daily Monday through Friday. Check the *www.JamesDicks.com* Web site for more information or listen to the radio show streamed live via the Internet. Come join me and ask your questions online. I look forward to your questions.

FIGURE 5-2   4X Made Easy Trading Screen

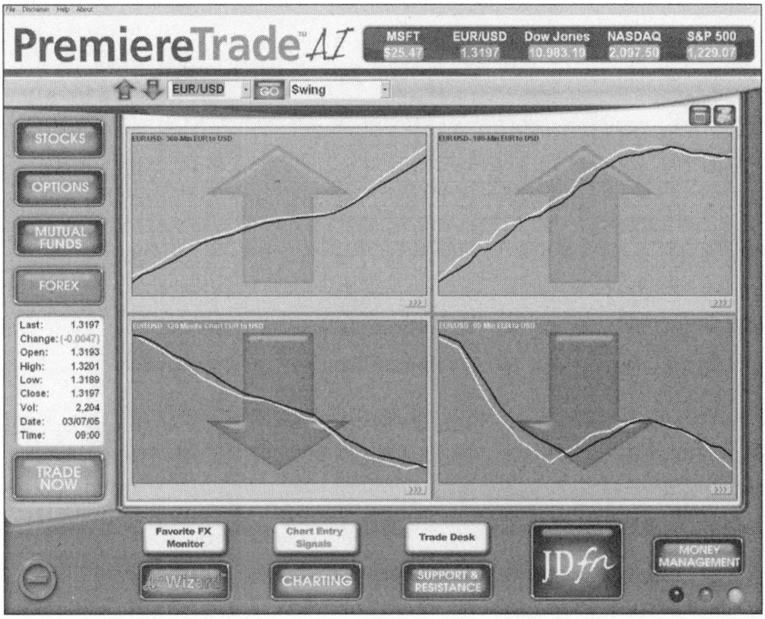

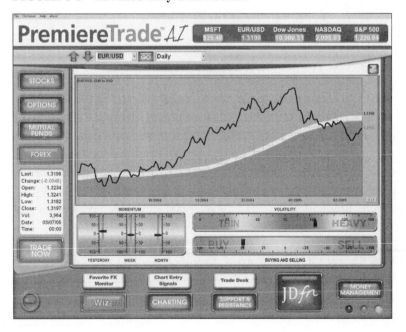

FIGURE 5-3   4X Made Easy Chart Screen

FIGURE 5-4   4X Made Easy Trade Vault

You can also go to *www.premieretrade.com* where there is live and archived online training for the FOREX and other investment subjects every day.

There are, of course, many other books to choose from, just not a lot about the FOREX. The more you read, the better it will be for your trading experience. A little secret from my past experience to note: First, all financial markets have inherent risk. You will not make money on every trade no matter what you use to trade with or how well you can trade. Trading is not a sprint but a marathon.

I have always believed that winning is contagious, whether hitting a baseball, trading, or whatever you may do. If you are placing trades and you are winning on all your trades, take advantage of that and make some money.

The same holds true when you make a bad trade and lose money. If it continues, take a step back, go for a walk, turn off the computer, and come back later. I know traders who will log off their real accounts and log onto a demo account and trade their demo account until they start making winning trades again. Whatever you do, just remember that it is a marathon.

C H A P T E R

FUNDAMENTALS OF TRADING

INTRODUCTION TO TRADING THEORY

The trading maxim "The trend is your friend" is as true today as it has ever been. The foreign exchange market (the FOREX) has long been recognized as one of the most consistently trending markets of all. There are trend-following opportunities for every trading time horizon. Look at a weekly or daily chart of any major cross-rate, and you will see trends that last several days, weeks, months, or even a year or more.

Technical traders have long acknowledged the value of market trends in profitable trading. As far back as the early 1900s, successful traders wrote about trends. Here is a quotation from one such early text, *Reminiscences of a Stock Operator,* by Edwin Lefevre. *Reminiscences of a Stock Operator* (John Wiley & Sons, Inc., New York, First Pub. 1923, this ed. 1994). This is the story of Jesse Livermore and was first printed in 1923. It is still considered to be a classic and a must read.

> I began to realize that the big money must necessarily be in the big swing. Whatever might seem to give a big swing its initial impulse, the fact is that its continuance is not the result of manipulations by pools or artifice by financiers, but depends upon basic conditions. And no matter who opposes it, the swing must inevitably run as far, and as fast, and as long as the impelling forces determine.
>
> Obviously the thing to do was to be bullish in a bull market and bearish in a bear market. Sounds silly, doesn't it? It took me a long time to grasp that general principle firmly before I saw that to put it into practice really meant to anticipate probabilities.

Despite the universal acceptance of this concept, despite the historical and experiential proof that it is the single most profitable trading tool, and despite the ease with which one can spot an ongoing trend and a reversal (the inception of a new trend), doing so remains the most difficult thing for most traders to do. Why? I believe that the problem is often two-sided, in that it is most likely a combination of psychological and technical deficiencies to varying degrees, depending on the individual trader's system application. This is the impediment that makes it so difficult to use trends in the profit-taking formula.

The psychological side may involve excessive fear, greed, or both. The technical-deficiency side may be a failure to learn a trading system well or not having the patience and discipline to execute it flawlessly.

TRENDS DEFINED

Price trends are market conditions in which price movement is consistently rising or falling. The market condition *opposite* to trends is a sideways market in which highs and lows are approximately the same levels.

A *trendline* is a straight line joining a series of price tops or bottoms that represents an area of support or resistance. Generally speaking, a reversal in a trend or a slowing down of the pace of a trend is indicated when the trendline is penetrated significantly. Trendlines should connect bottoms on a rising graph and tops on a falling graph (see Figure 6-1).

Interpretation

There are several points to consider in judging the penetration of a trendline. The number of times the price touches the trendline is significant. The larger the number, the greater is the support or resistance. The length of the trend is important. If the series of tops or bottoms covers only 3 to 4 weeks, the trendline is a minor one, and penetration is of little importance. However, if the trend covers several months or years, penetration of the trendline is viewed as a major occurrence. The violation of a very steep trendline is of less importance than that of a slower, more gradual one.

TREND CYCLES

Markets are in a constant state of balance and imbalance. They make impulse moves and then correction moves. We may refer to these moves as *waves*. We will see *impulse waves* and *correction waves* as markets move in trends. When market prices are flat, they usually have reached a temporary state of equilibrium.

While we look for trends on a long-interval chart, every trend consists of smaller price movements or waves. These smaller price movements can be categorized in order to identify the highest probability wave in which to trade with the trend.

These market conditions include *channel breakout, vector (strong) trend, countertrend, weak trend*, and *nontrend*. Whether you look at a long-interval chart or a short-interval chart, you will find all these market conditions to one degree or another.

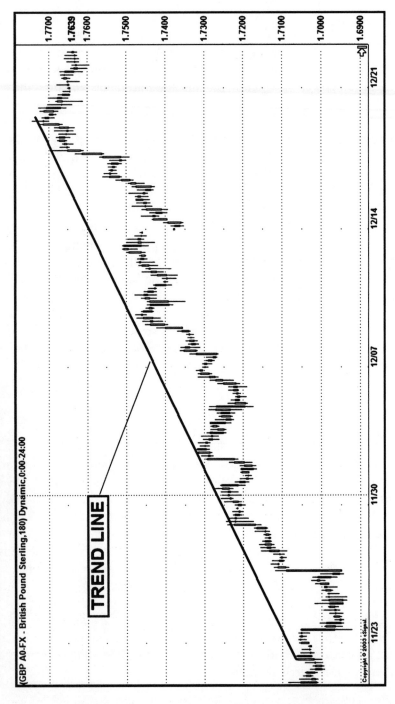

FIGURE 6-1 GBP/USD 180-Minute Chart 2002–2003

HIGH-PROBABILITY TRADING

The highest probability trading will be in agreement with the *strong-trend* portion of the trendline found on a *long-interval chart* and then using shorter-interval charts to find preferred entry and exit zones for trades. In short, this is *continuance trading*: finding an established trend and trading the *continuance*, or waves, of that trend.

Therefore, the best strategy is to trade continuances in agreement with the underlying trend or swing found on long-interval charts. If the market is thrusting up, *buy dips*. If the market is thrusting down, *sell rallies*.

SIDEWAYS, NONTREND STRATEGY: WAIT FOR STRONG TRENDS

Generally speaking, I avoid trading in *narrow* sideways trends. If you observe a *wide* sideways trend on a long-interval chart, where smaller trends are found moving from the bottom of the sideways range to the top and then from the top down to the bottom, it is possible, with some qualification, to trade those moves using short-interval charts.

On a short-interval chart, these moves appear as short trend moves oscillating between a distinguishable top and bottom price range (See Figure 6-2).

UPTREND TRADING STRATEGY: BUY AT DIP BOTTOMS

As with all strategies it is how you manage it that counts. A strategy that works in upward trending markets is buying on the dips at the bottoms. What I mean by this is that nothing goes straight up, often times you will see a stock or position go up and then start to recycle, with a reverse or profit taking.

If the position is going up nicely and you are looking at a price chart you will see the bars (up-ticks) continue to move upwards. If you see the price chart all of a sudden start to move in the downward range you have a change in direction. Look at Figure 6-3. If we say that this is a daily price chart then each one of the bars black or white represent a day's worth of trading activity.

So in this case you will see that the position has an long-term trend of moving up. Along the way a few road bumps. In this example you really do not see any trend reversals, this is when the price chart will actually show the position heading as much down if not more than upward.

FIGURE 6-2 GBP/USD 180-Minute Chart 2003

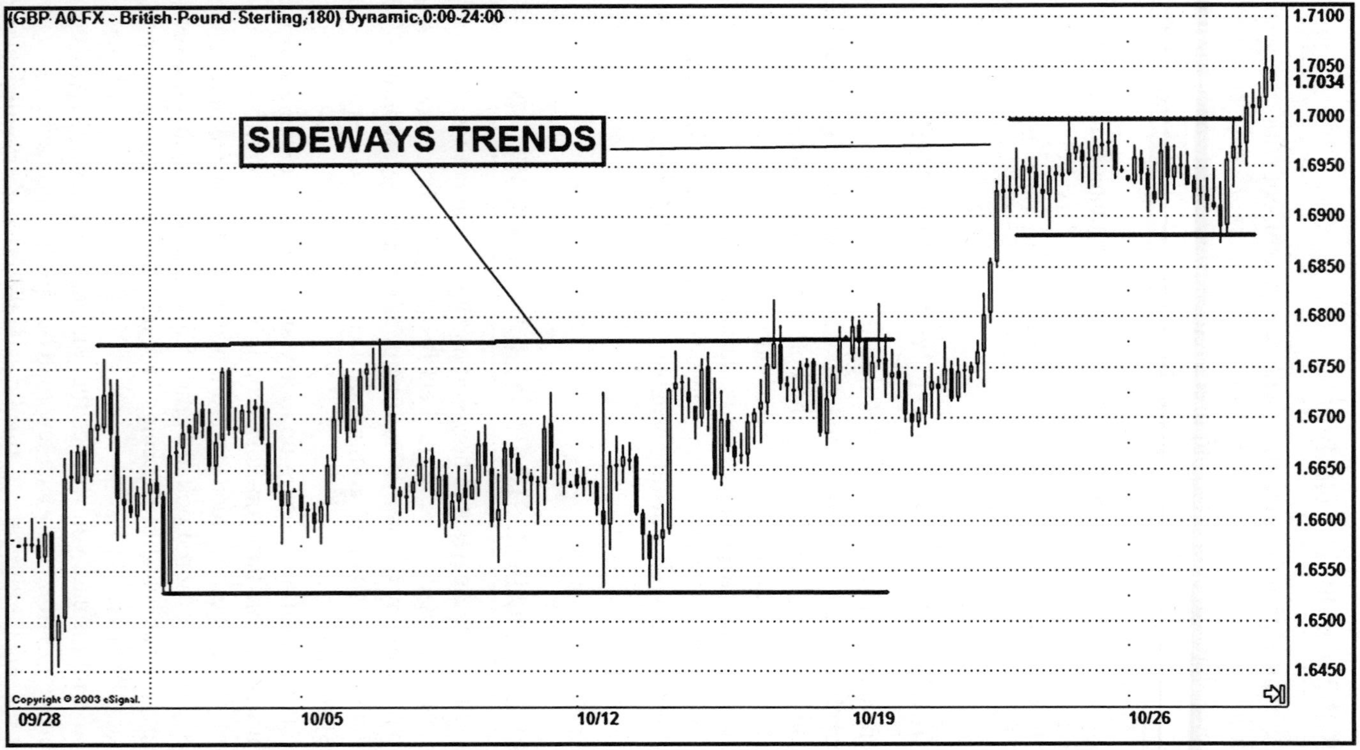

(GBP A0-FX - British Pound-Sterling,180) Dynamic,0:00-24:00

SIDEWAYS TRENDS

Copyright © 2003 eSignal.

1.7100
1.7050
1.7034
1.7000
1.6950
1.6900
1.6850
1.6800
1.6750
1.6700
1.6650
1.6600
1.6550
1.6500
1.6450

09/28   10/05   10/12   10/19   10/26

If you look at Figure 6-3 you will see from left to right that the position is consolidating or moving sideways. Often times when you see a position moving sideways and it is at the bottom of the screen the position is looking for direction. Usually the position will go up from here. Consolidation of moving sideways is just that. The overall direction of the bars or daily price is really not going up or down but just kind of sitting there in a range. A range is when the position is say going up to 12 dollars and down to 10 dollars but no further away up or down from those prices.

When you see the consolidation happening at the top of the chart it is usually looking for direction and is often times overbought and will move in a downward direction. Overbought is when you have to many buyers and no sellers. Now there is no more room for it to go up and no one is selling. A shift will usually take place in the direction as profit taking will kick in.

Profit taking is just that investors start taking their profits because the position has gone up nicely over a period of time say daily, weekly, monthly, or yearly. Let's look at figure 6-3 again and follow along form left to right again. You will see the consolidation period (sideways) movement and then the position finds direction; the buyers start to buy more than the sellers are willing to sell and you have the supply and demand game. That drives the price up until it hits resistance. Often times investors miss the first opportunity to get in on the position when it takes off from its consolidation period.

So you have the first run up and profit taking kicks in. The buyers start selling and the sellers start to outweigh the buyers and the position starts to go down. If it is just normal profit taking the position will go down looking for some support. The support is simply where the buyers think there is a good deal and start buying again. We will cover support in more detail. All of a sudden you have more buying than selling and the position starts to go up again; at this point you will see the chart start to move back in a positive direction. It is at this time a dip has occurred and you have an additional opportunity to buy back in.

Now looking in Figure 6-3 you will see a long run-up period were the position just looks like it is going straight up. There really are no opportunities to get back in as there are no definable dips in the price. And if you look at the top just to the left you will see that as the position seems to have hit some resistance it starts to consolidate a bit. The price moves sideways. Some investors will see this as a small dip in price and an opportunity to get in the position. What usually happens is that the position will move up slightly and then correct a bit before going back up.

The difference between profit taking and correction is that profit taking is usually only for a brief period and the position will move down toward its near term support (not very far from its last high). A correction is where the position has run up pretty strong and then turned around significantly not enough to change the overall direction of the trend but enough to give back a large portion of your profits. This is one reason that I really talk about money management. Good money management will protect your downside when the position goes into a correction. A correction can be classified as a percentage of the last move up to what it can be expected to go down. So if the position goes up say 10 dollars and then goes back down 5 dollars before going back up again you would have had a 50 percent retracement.

So buying on dips gives an investor numerous opportunities to add to their positions or get in on the trade.

Figure 6-3 illustrates this concept.

DOWNTREND TRADING STRATEGY: SELL AT RALLY TOPS

Selling on rallies is really the exact opposite of buying on dips. The trend is going down instead of going up. When the position starts to move upward it is retracing, or profit taking just in the opposite way as the previous example showed. So when the position moves up and starts to go back down you can add to your positions on the short side. Going short is just selling before you buy.

In the FOREX it is a little different than shorting a stock. You are only taking the other side of the trade. Say you were looking at the EUR/USD. If you wanted to short it, you would say sell. This is what you would do if you thought the U.S. dollar was going to get stronger. Essentially what you are doing is really buying dollars and selling euros. So as not to confuse you just think of it as buying and selling. When the EUR/USD is going up, you buy and when the EUR/USD is going down, you sell.

Figure 6-4 illustrates this strategy.

SYMMETRICAL TRIANGLE

The *symmetrical triangle* is the most prevalent of the triangle patterns. It may be considered to be both bearish and bullish and is found in both uptrends and downtrends.

One difference from other triangle patterns is that the breakout likely can go either way but usually aligns with the prevailing trend, as opposed to bullish ascending triangles or bearish descending triangles.

FIGURE 6-3 EUR/USD Daily Chart 2002–2003

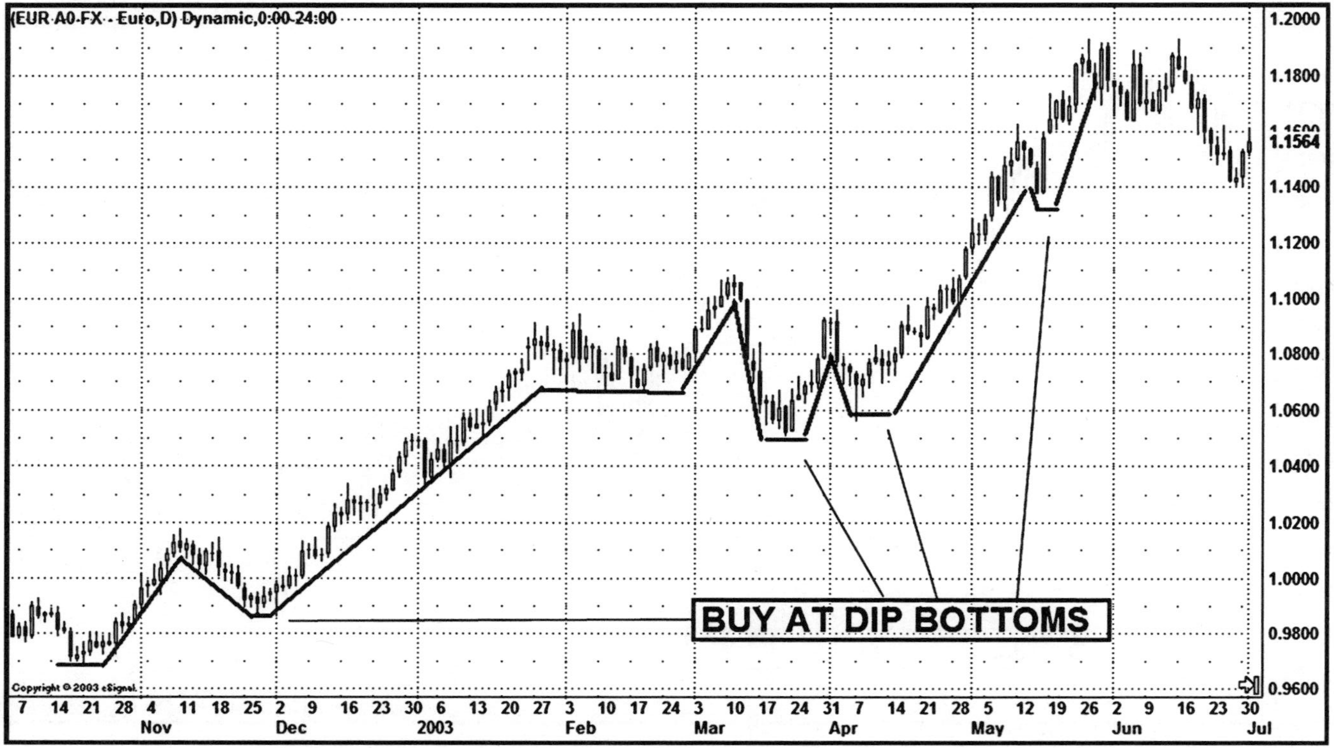

FIGURE 6-4   USD/CHF 180-Minute Chart 2002–2003

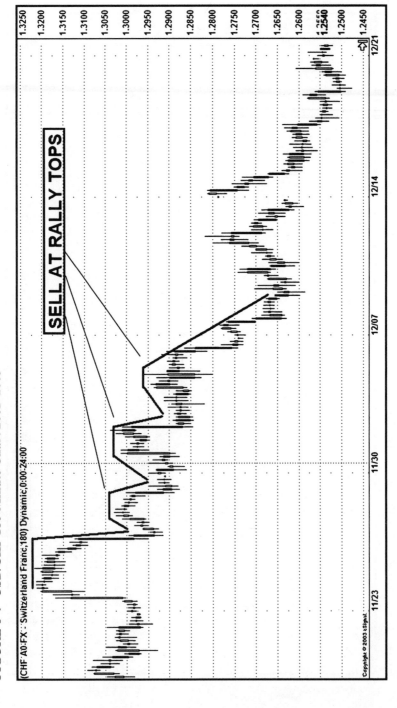

The symmetrical triangle is a formation that is also considered a consolidation period. Sometimes in a downtrend or uptrend it acts as a midpoint to a continuation of the pattern.

Sometimes symmetrical triangles even form as reversal patterns at the end of a trend, but typically they are continuation patterns. Regardless of where they form, symmetrical triangles are patterns worthy of watching because they indicate that buyers or sellers are at a standstill and waiting for a catalyst that could make the currency pair break out to higher or lower prices in the short term.

RULES OF THE SYMMETRICAL TRIANGLE
Figure 6-5 illustrates the rules of the symmetrical triangle.

Trend. Found both in an uptrend and a downtrend.

Shape. The bottom trendline placed across at least two points must make an upward-sloping line. The lows do not have to be a whole lot higher but should be noticeably higher than others (so others will see it also). There should be a few days to a few months between the proximal lows. The upper descending trendline is formed by at least two high points connected by a trendline that angles downward and to the right. These highs should be successively lower, and there also should be a few days to a few months distance between the lows. There must be at least four points touching the trendlines, but there can be many more than four total.

Duration. The length of the pattern can range from a few weeks to many months, with the average pattern lasting from 1 to 3 months.

Volume. As the pattern develops, volume usually contracts. When the downside breakout occurs, there is usually stronger volume to confirm the breakout, but this is not always necessary. In the FOREX, you are watching the volume of lots traded. This is seen on most software and charting tools, including eSignal.

Pullback. Following the breakdown or breakout, the currency pair usually will rebound back up to previous support or resistance. On a breakdown, what was the lower trendline support turns into resistance, and vice versa. In symmetrical triangles, the pullback occurs with more than 21 percent of the breaks, with 16 percent falling back into the symmetrical triangle formation as a false move, and sometimes will change direction totally. You can use the apex of the trendlines as a stop-loss price.

FIGURE 6-5 Symmetrical Triangle

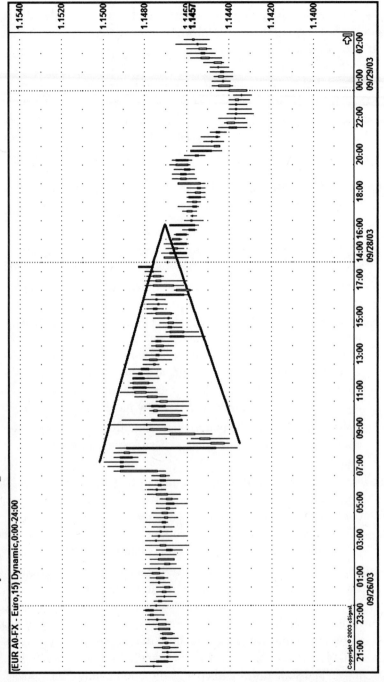

Target. Once the breakout has occurred, the price projection is found by measuring the widest distance of the pattern at the first confirmation point and adding it to the breakout price.

ASCENDING TRIANGLE: A BULLISH CONTINUATION PATTERN

The *ascending triangle* is a bullish formation that usually forms during an uptrend as a continuation pattern. Sometimes an ascending triangle forms as a reversal pattern at the end of a downtrend, but typically it is a bullish continuation pattern. Regardless of where ascending triangles form, they are bullish patterns that indicate that buyers are accumulating the currency pair, and it could break out to higher prices in the short term.

RULES OF THE ASCENDING TRIANGLE

Figure 6-6 illustrates the rules of the ascending triangle.

Trend. Usually it forms in an uptrend.

Shape. The top trendline placed across at least two points must make a horizontal line. The highs do not have to be exact but should be within reasonable proximity of each other. There should be a few days to a few months between the proximal highs. The lower ascending trendline is formed by at least two low points connected by a trendline that angles upward and to the right. These lows should be successively higher, and there also should be a few days to a few months distance between the lows. There must be at least four points touching the trendlines, but there can be many more than four total.

Duration. The length of the pattern can range from a few weeks to many months, with the average pattern lasting from 1 to 3 months.

Volume. As the pattern develops, volume usually contracts. When the upside breakout occurs, there is usually stronger volume to confirm the breakout, but this is not always necessary.

Throwback. Following the breakout, the currency pair usually will pull back to support. On a breakout, what was the upper trendline resistance turns into support, and vice versa. Sometimes there will be a return to this support level before the move begins again. This is called the *throwback.* You can use the upper trendline support as a tight stop loss and the rising lower trendline as a hard stop.

FIGURE 6-6 Ascending triangle

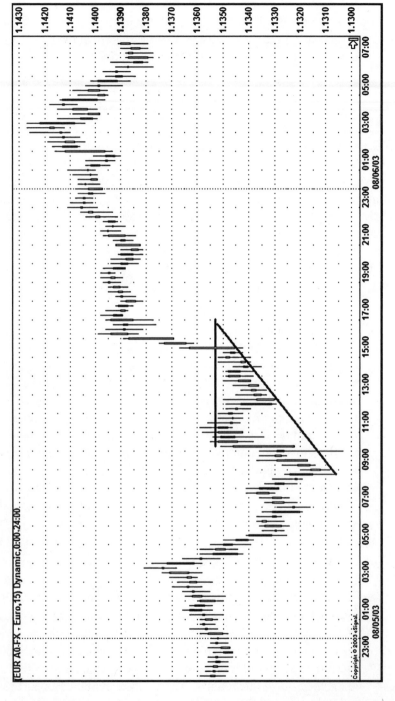

Target. Once the breakout has occurred, the price projection is found by measuring the widest distance of the pattern at the first confirmation point and adding it to the resistance breakout price.

DESCENDING TRIANGLE

The *descending triangle,* also a variation of the symmetrical triangle, generally is considered to be bearish and usually is found in downtrends. The ascending triangle is a bullish formation that usually forms during an uptrend as a continuation pattern. Sometimes descending triangles form as reversal patterns at the end of a downtrend, but typically they are bullish continuation patterns. Regardless of where they form, descending triangles are bullish patterns that indicate that buyers are accumulating the currency pair and that it could break out to higher prices in the short term.

RULES OF THE DESCENDING TRIANGLE
Figure 6-7 illustrates the rules of the descending triangle.

Trend. Usually it forms in a downtrend.

Shape. The bottom trendline placed across at least two points must make a horizontal line. The highs do not have to be exact but should be within reasonable proximity of each other. There should be a few days to a few months between the proximal lows. The upper descending trendline is formed by at least two low points connected by a trendline that angles downward and to the right. These highs should be successively lower, and there also should be a few days to a few months' distance between the lows. There must be at least four points touching the trendlines, but there can be many more than four total.

Duration. The length of the pattern can range from a few weeks to many months, with the average pattern lasting from 1 to 3 months.

Volume. As the pattern develops, volume usually contracts. When the downside breakout occurs, there is usually stronger volume to confirm the breakout, but this is not always necessary.

Pullback. Following the breakdown, the currency pair usually will rebound back up to previous support. On a breakdown, what was the lower trendline support turns into resistance, and vice versa. Sometimes there will be a return to this resistance level

FIGURE 6-7 Descending triangle

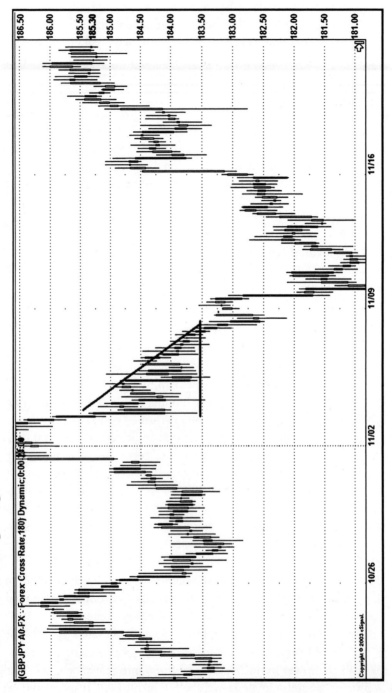

before the down move resumes. This is called the *pullback.* In
descending triangles, the pullback occurs with more than 23
percent of the breakdowns, with 12 percent falling back into the
descending triangle formation and moving upward. You can use
the lower trendline resistance as a tight cover point if you are
short or the falling upper trendline as a hard stop.

Target. Once the breakout has occurred, the price projection is found
by measuring the widest distance of the pattern at the first confirmation point and adding it to the resistance breakdown price.

THE FALLING BROADENING FORMATION

The *falling broadening formation* is similar to a megaphone in appearance,
in that it has diverging trendlines that spread apart from an apex. These are
generally distinguished by a noticeable slant to the downside.

A falling broadening formation generally is considered bearish and
usually is found in short-term downtrends or at the midpoint of an uptrend.
The implication, however, is still generally bearish. This pattern is marked
by a series of lower tops and lower bottoms.

The currency typically will bounce off the lower trendline and retrace
from the upper trendline. Once the currency pair breaks out above the
upper trendline, the pattern can be considered a reversal, and the uptrend
should resume.

SUPPORT BREAKDOWN OR RESISTANCE BREAKOUT

Understanding support and resistance is a very important part of charting
to save losses, hold on for gains, and preserve capital. *Support* refers to the
price level at which a security tends to stop falling because there is more
demand than supply. Technical analysts identify support levels as prices at
which a particular currency pair has bottomed in the past.

When a currency pair is falling toward its support level, it is said to be
"testing its support," meaning that the currency pair should rebound as
soon as it hits the support price. If the currency pair continues to drop
through the support level, its outlook is considered very bearish. When support is broken, it often defines a new resistance point.

A *support breakdown* refers to a currency pair's previous level of support. Once this level is broken, the currency pair typically will fall to its

next support level. Technical tools used to determine support levels such as trendlines and the Fibonacci fan frequently will forewarn or suggest that a major downtrend or consolidation period is ahead.

Resistance refers to the price ceiling at which currency pairs reach persistent selling. It is significant when a currency pair breaks through the resistance level because this means that it usually will go on to new highs. When resistance is broken, it often defines a new support level.

A *breakout* refers to a currency pair emerging up through a previous resistance level and usually to a new high. It is significant when the currency pair breaks through the resistance level, in that the volume is increasing because this means it usually will go on to new highs.

When resistance is broken, it often defines a new support level. If the volume is weaker than normal on the breakout, the move higher usually will be short-lived due to a lack of broad participation.

THE DOUBLE BOTTOM

The *double bottom* is a formation in which a currency pair hits a low, rallies, and then falls back to the low. Usually this is a bullish formation that precedes an up move and is an important formation when identifying an entry point. The shape of the pattern is much like the letter *W* in that the currency pair will make two important lows within near price proximity of each other.

If the price breaks below the two low points, the pattern is void, and the currency pair could continue lower.

Typically, the currency pair will move higher off the second low and continue to break out above the left arm of the *W*. At this point the breakout and the formation are complete, and the currency pair should continue higher to a target at least equal to that of the height of the formation.

RULES OF THE DOUBLE BOTTOM
Figure 6-8 illustrates the rules of the double bottom.

Trend. Found both in uptrends and downtrends but more prevalent in downtrends.

Shape. Much like that of the letter *W*, and the formation is completed when the price goes above the left arm of the *W*. There must be two low points in close price proximity of each other.

Duration. The length of the pattern can range from a few minutes to many.

FIGURE 6-8 Double Bottom Support

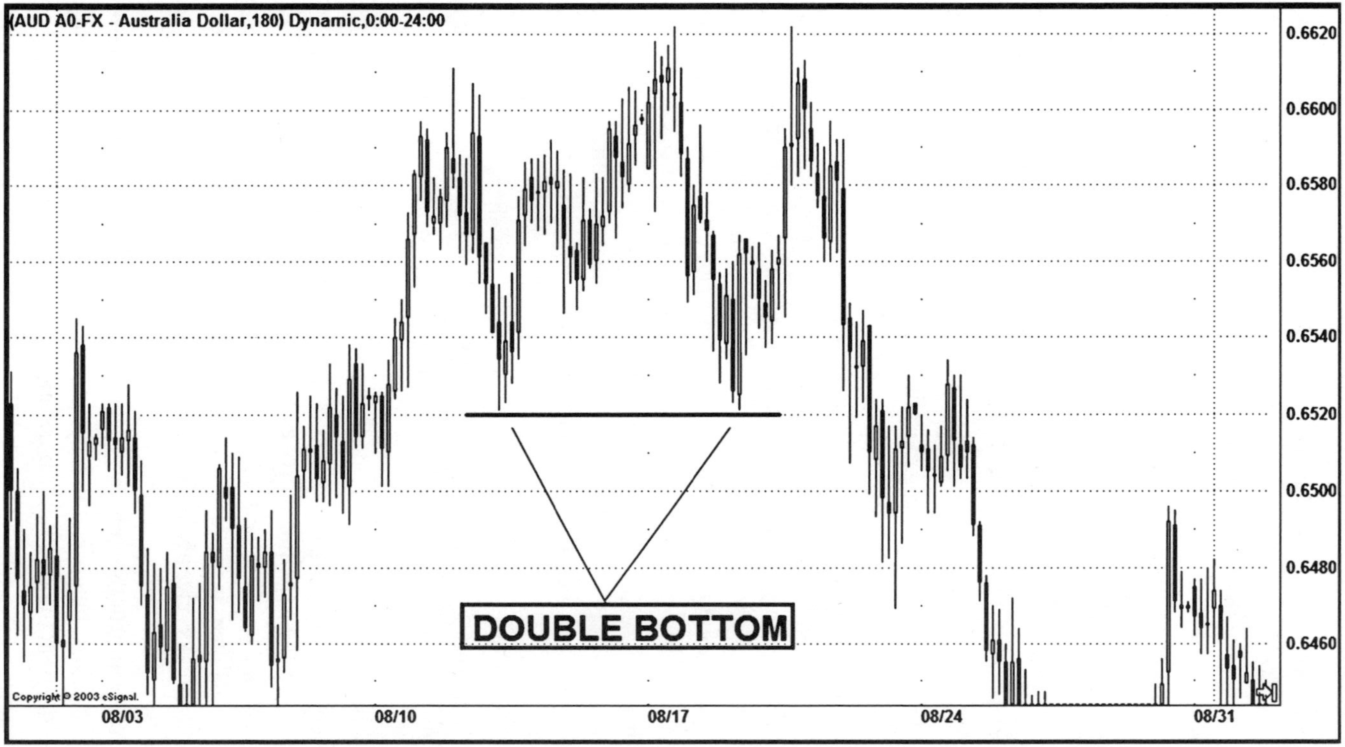

(AUD A0-FX - Australia Dollar,180) Dynamic,0:00-24:00

DOUBLE BOTTOM

Copyright © 2003 eSignal.

08/03   08/10   08/17   08/24   08/31

0.6620
0.6600
0.6580
0.6560
0.6540
0.6520
0.6500
0.6480
0.6460

Volume. As the pattern develops, volume usually contracts. When the breakout occurs, there is usually stronger volume to confirm the breakout, but this is not always necessary.

Target. Once the breakout has occurred, the price projection is found by measuring the height of the pattern and adding it to the break-out price.

HEAD AND SHOULDERS (CROWN)

A *head and shoulders* is a formation that usually precedes a sell-off. The head and shoulders pattern generally is regarded as a reversal pattern and is seen most often in uptrends. It is also most reliable when found in an uptrend (see Figure 6-9).

A rebound that is strong will begin to slow down eventually. About the same time, supply and demand are generally in balance. Sellers come in at the highs (left shoulder), and the downside begins (beginning neckline).

Buyers soon return to the currency pair and ultimately push through to new highs. However, the new highs are quickly turned back, and the down-side is tested again (continuing neckline).

Reduced buying reemerges, and the currency pair rallies once more but fails to take out the existing top level. (This last top is considered the right shoulder.)

Buying dries up, and the currency pair tests the downside yet again. Your trend line for this pattern should be drawn from the beginning neck-line to the continuing neckline. In this case, the neckline is descending, which is even more negative.

Volume has a greater importance in the head and shoulders pattern in comparison with other patterns and generally decreases as the pattern is built. Once the neckline is broken, the currency pair frequently will sell off an equal distance from the neckline to the head.

In this case it could reach 1700. The pattern is completed when the market breaks the neckline, as we saw in the figure. (Volume should increase on the breakout.)

Are you watching out for *reversal bars?* You should be. The next time you see a currency pair down in the morning and then reverse to end up or unchanged on the day, don't blow it off as a nonevent. Take a closer look.

Reversal bars come in two different forms. One version is a *churning bar,* in which a currency pair's opening price and closing price are close to or equal to the same price.

FIGURE 6-9　Head and Shoulders

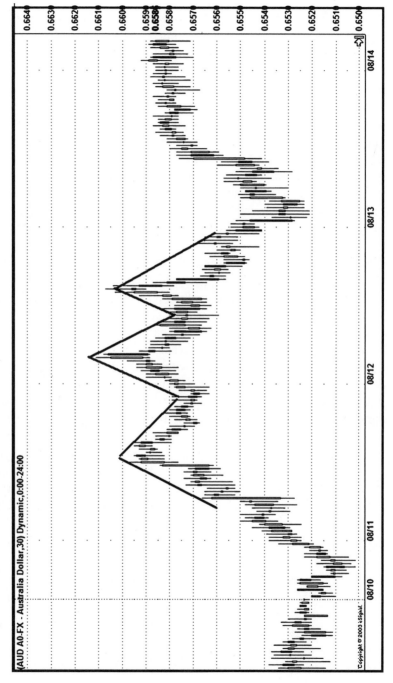

71

There can be a wide price range during the day, but it ends up closing near where it opened. These days frequently go unnoticed by a novice. Following a big move or if the volume is anything but light, take a close look.

The second version is a *key reversal,* which again follows a short-term trend in a currency pair. Then a day presents itself when the market moves big in the same direction in the morning but then reverses to close well below the currency pair's previous close in an uptrend or well above the currency pair's previous close in a downtrend.

The psychology behind this kind of bar is that buyers and sellers are pouring into the particular currency pair with equal enthusiasm and essentially run out of steam. If the currency pair is in an uptrend, the buyers run out of new money or buying power, so the currency pair will then fall bringing pressure to the sellers that are out there, and the currency pair can retrace without any real selling pressure.

The same happens in a downtrend. If the currency pair has been selling off recently and you see a churning bar on high volume, this could be a bottom. The buyers are coming in and soaking up all the sellers. Therefore, the buyers in the future can move the currency pair higher without much overhead selling pressure. The currency pair can then move higher until the "churning buyers" get enough profits to start selling themselves.

There are many different strategies with which you can trade. I only covered a few simple rules that many professional traders follow. Most professional traders take these same techniques and refine them to their very own trading styles. As we are all different, in our lives and financial needs,we have to tailor our investing to our own specific needs. You can learn how to trade following some of the guide lines we just discussed or you can create your own. You could even use one of the many trading software out there to help you trade. Regardless of how you decide to trade remember this, confirmation, confirmation, confirmation. I love to say this as you can never have too much confirmation before placing a trade.

C H A P T E R

7

ECONOMIC FUNDAMENTALS

INTRODUCTION

Any news that has a bearing on the economy, whether directly or indirectly, is considered fundamental. This news may include the changes in the economy, changes to interest rates, political elections, and natural disasters. In order to allow navigation through the changing universe of fundamentals, news is classified into one of four categories: economic factors, financial factors, political factors, and crises.

Not only will economic data differ among counties, but their importance, timing, and dates of release also differ. Economic data usually are scheduled for release in advance, and times and dates of releases are easily available, at least in the industrialized nations.

Political factors, unlike economic data, vary in terms of dates and times and certainly have a huge impact on the foreign exchange market (the FOREX). The U.S. market is more stable than those of other countries because most elections occur every 4 years and new nominations are announced to the public in advance.

In other countries, such as Italy, governments are less stable, and the timing of parliamentary elections cannot be forecasted in advance. To the extreme side, we can look to the fall of the Soviet Union, the new future of Iraq, and the political tensions between France and Germany and the United States.

Financial factors are partially timed and predicted. Discount rates are changed by central banks such as the Federal Reserve (Fed) in the United States, the European Central Bank (ECB), and Bank of Japan (BOJ), and although the changes in rates are kept in high secrecy, markets watch closely and make their predictions in advance. While rate changes are mostly unknown in advance, the dates that the central banks meet are available in the financial news.

A crisis may or may not have a huge impact on a country's currency. Most recently, while Allied forces entered Iraq, the U.S. dollar saw little change as the war started and ended, but the kidnapping of Mikhail Gorbachev, then president of the Soviet Union, had a sharp effect on the FOREX.

ECONOMIC INDICATORS

Economic indicators by far provide the most information of all the fundamental factors. Unlike the financial, political, and crisis factors, economic factors occur in a steady stream, at certain times, and more often. It is extremely important for you to be aware of these economic announcements so that you can to make informed decisions on entering, exiting, or adjusting your positions.

Traders around the world have their eyes glued to their monitors when economic data are announced, but knowing when these announcements are to be made is only half the battle. Forecasting the proper trend will generate true profits.

ECONOMIC DATA RELEASE

Economic data generally are released on a monthly basis, except the gross domestic product (GDP) and the employment cost index (ECI), which are released quarterly. While several indicators are released weekly, very few have an impact on the FOREX. All indicators are announced in pairs.

The first number is the new number, and the second one is the pervious number for comparison. It is important to remember that most reports are released between 8:30 and 10:00 A.M. (EST).

SOURCES OF INFORMATION

Information about upcoming economic indicators is available in all the leading newspapers, such as the *Wall Street Journal*, the *Financial Times*, and the *New York Times*. While newspapers are a great resource, it seems that the Internet is still where many traders turn for information. Trusted Web sites include http://money.cnn.com, http://www.bloomberg.com, and http://moneycentral.msn.com/investor/home.asp. Another good source is to go to the New York Federal Reserve Bank Web site at http://www.ny.frb.org/. All have economic indicators and a calendar for upcoming announcements.

THE GROSS NATIONAL PRODUCT (GNP) AND
GROSS DOMESTIC PRODUCT (GDP)

The GNP is said to be the most significant economic indicator, and many analysts agree that it strongly measures economic performance as a whole. GNP is the sum of all goods and services produced by U.S. residents both in the United States and abroad.

On the other hand, the GDP refers to the sum of all goods and services produced in the United States by both domestic and foreign companies. The GDP figures are more popular outside the United States.

CONSUMER SPENDING

Consumer spending is more psychological in nature and measures consumer confidence rather than actual spending. Consumer spending is made possible by personal income and discretionary income, so consumer confidence is important for those who have discretional income in order to switch to buying from saving.

GOVERNMENT SPENDING

Government spending is very important in that its sheer size and impact on the economy are tremendous, but it is also very influential in other ways. Due to special expenditures such as military spending, it boosts the unemployment rate and GDP and promotes investment spending.

INFLATION INDICATORS

The rate of inflation is the rise in overall prices, and gauging inflation is a vital macroeconomic task. Traders watch inflation very closely because one of the ways to fight inflation is by raising interest rates. Higher interest rates tend to support the local currency.

Values of the real interest rate and real GNP and GDP are of the most importance to money managers and traders, allowing them to accurately compare the worldwide market. Generally, traders use nine economic tools:

- Producer price index (PPI)

- Purchasing managers' index (PMI)

- Consumer price index (CPI)

- Durable goods

- GNP deflator

- GDP deflator

- Employment cost index (ECI)

- Commodity Research Bureau's index (CRB index)

- *Journal of Commerce* industrial price index (JoC index)

PRODUCER PRICE INDEX (PPI)

The PPI has been compiled since the beginning of the twentieth century and was called the *wholesale price index* until 1978. The PPI gauges the average changes in prices received by domestic producers for their output at all stages of processing.

Unlike the CPI, which includes imported goods, services, and taxes, the PPI compiles from sectors such as manufacturing, mining, and agriculture. Calculation of the PPI involves around 3400 commodities.

PURCHASING MANAGERS' INDEX (PMI)

The National Association of Purchasing Managers (NAPM), now renamed the Institute for Supply Management, releases a monthly composite index of national manufacturing conditions constructed from data on new orders, production, supplier delivery times, backlogs, inventories, prices, employment, export orders, and import orders. It is divided into manufacturing and nonmanufacturing subindices.

CONSUMER PRICE INDEX (CPI)

The CPI gauges the average change in retail prices for a fixed market of goods and services. The CPI is compiled from a sample of prices for food, shelter, clothing, fuel, transportation, and medical services that people purchase on a daily basis.

Both indexes, the PPI and the CPI, are of great help to investors in determining whether the economy is in an inflationary state, and both numbers are announced monthly.

DURABLE GOODS

Durable goods orders measure new orders placed with domestic manufacturers for immediate and future delivery of factory hard goods. A *durable good* is defined as a good that lasts an extended period of time (over 3 years) during which its services are extended.

GNP DEFLATOR

The GNP figure is not helpful to traders by itself. A large number may or may not be good for the economy, depending on the level of inflation. Therefore, the nominal GNP figure must be deflated by some price index.

There are several GNP deflators, but the most commonly used is the *implicit deflator.* The implicit deflator is calculated by dividing the current-dollar GNP figure by the constant-dollar GNP figure.

GDP DEFLATOR

The same holds true for the GDP deflator as for the GNP deflator. Both the GNP and GDP implicit deflators are released quarterly, along with respective GNP and GDP numbers. The implicit deflators generally are regarded as the most significant measure of inflation.

COMMODITY RESEARCH BUREAU'S FUTURES INDEX (CRB INDEX)

The CRB index makes determining inflationary trends easier. The CRB index consists of equally weighted futures prices of 21 commodities. The components of the CRB index are

- Precious metals: gold, silver, and platinum

- Industrials: crude oil, heating oil, unleaded gas, lumber, copper, and cotton

- Grains: corn, wheat, soybeans, soy meal, and soy oil

- Livestock and meat: cattle, hops, and pork bellies
- Imports: coffee, cocoa, and sugar
- Miscellaneous: orange juice

The CRB index has been a popular tool that has proven reliable since the late 1980s.

THE JoC INDUSTRIAL PRICE INDEX
The JoC index was designed to signal changes in inflation prior to other price indexes. The JoC index consists of the prices of 18 industrial materials and supplies processed in the initial stages of manufacturing, building, and energy production.

EMPLOYMENT INDICATORS

The employment rate is an economic indicator that is significant in the FOREX because of it importance to forecast in multiple economic areas. The employment rate normally measures the stability and soundness of an economy. In addition, however, the indicator is used as a major component in calculation of the GNP and GDP.

In the FOREX, the standard indicators studied by traders are the unemployment rate, manufacturing payrolls, nonfarm payrolls, average earnings, and average workweek. Generally, the most significant data come from manufacturing and nonfarm payrolls, followed by the unemployment rate. These data are released on a monthly basis.

CONSUMER SPENDING INDICATORS

RETAIL SALES
Retail sales are an important indicator because they show the strength of consumer demand as well as consumer confidence. In the United States, this indicator is more important than in other countries such as Japan because the U.S. economy is more focused on consumers.

A higher retail sales figure creates an economic process of forward motion in the manufacturing sector. Some months are significant for this indicator to show positive figures. Those months are September, November, and December.

The first month of the three signifies a back-to-school and back-to-work month. November and December are holiday shopping months, and traders look closely at pre-December to post-Christmas data.

CONSUMER SENTIMENT

Consumer sentiment is a survey of households that is designed to measure individuals' tendency for spending. The University of Michigan and the National Family Opinion Conference Board conduct the two studies in this area. The index measured by the Conference Board is sensitive to the job market, whereas that of the University of Michigan is not.

HOUSING STARTS

The housing starts report measures the number of residential units on which construction has begun each month. A *start* in construction is defined as the beginning of excavation of the foundation for the building, and the measure consists primarily of residential housing. Housing is very interest-rate sensitive and is one of the first sectors to react to changes in interest rates. Significant reaction of start/permits to changing interest rates signals that interest rates are nearing a trough or peak. To analyze, focus on the percentage change in levels from the preceding month. The report is released around the middle of the following month.

AUTOMOBILE SALES

Although the U.S. economy relies on automobile sales in terms of production and retail sales, the level of automobile sales is not an indicator most FOREX traders follow too closely.

INDUSTRIAL PRODUCTION

This is a chain-weighted measure of the change in production in the nation's factories, mines, and utilities, as well as a measure of their industrial capacity and of how many available resources among factories, utilities, and mines are being used (commonly known as *capacity utilization*).

The manufacturing sector accounts for one-quarter of the economy. The capacity utilization rate provides an estimate of how much factory capacity is in use.

LEADING INDICATORS

The leading indicators consist of the following economic indicators:

- Average workweek of production workers in manufacturing

- Average weekly claims for state unemployment

- New orders for consumer goods and materials (adjusted for inflation)

- Vendor performance

- Contract and orders for plant and equipment

- New building permits issued

- Change in manufacturers' unfilled orders, durable goods

- Change in sensitive materials prices

- Index of stock prices

- Money supply, adjusted for inflation

- Index of consumer expectations

These indexes are designed to offer a 6- to 9-month future outlook of economic performance. These figures are also great tools to forecast inflation and deflation, and unlike the unemployment rate, which is a lagging indicator, these indicators are for a future outlook.

Unlike in the stock market, when news is released, the FOREX will react, especially the currency in question. Make sure that you know your news. There are many alert services out there to which you can subscribe that will help you with this.

Don't be too quick to pull the trigger should a particular economic indicator fall outside market expectations. Contained in each new economic indicator released to the public are revisions to previously released data. For example, if durable goods should rise by 0.5 percent in the current month and the market is anticipating them to fall, the unexpected rise could be the result of a downward revision of the figures for the prior month.

Look at revisions to older data because in such cases the preceding month's figure may have been reported originally as a rise of 0.5 percent but now, along with the new figures, is being revised lower to, say, a rise of only 0.1 percent Therefore, the unexpected rise in the current month is likely the result of a downward revision of the preceding month's data.

Be careful not to place a trade when major economic news is coming out because the FOREX can move very quickly. If you are going to place trades prior to news announcements, make sure that you are protected with a good stop loss.

8

INTRODUCTION TO TECHNICAL ANALYSIS

- Technical Analysis Defined
- Technical Analysis Assumptions
- Bar and Candlestick Charts
- Technical Analysis Terms
- Market Patterns: Up Trends, Down Trends, and Sideways Trends
- Support and Resistance

TECHNICAL ANALYSIS DEFINED

Before we begin an in-depth study of the PremiereTrade trading method, we must first define what technical analysis is for our purposes. *Technical analysis* is the study of historical and ongoing price data through charts, price patterns, and chart indicators. Charts display price in time intervals using bars or candlesticks.

TECHNICAL ANALYSIS ASSUMPTIONS

A repeat of the philosophical assumptions on which technical analysis is based is appropriate here before we begin the study of analyzing market patterns.

1.   All available information and its impact on traders and the market are already reflected in a currency's price.
2.   Prices move in trends or patterns.
3.   History repeats itself.

TECHNICAL ANALYSIS ALLOWS FOR AN INDIRECT STUDY OF ALL MARKET DATA, INCLUDING FUNDAMENTALS

Most technical traders (technicians) would agree that the underlying forces of supply and demand and the economic fundamentals of the market cause uptrends and downtrends. As a general rule, we are not going to concern ourselves so much with the reasons why market prices move up or down. Instead, we are going to discount the reasons why and are going to trade in agreement with the supporting technical indicators.

PRICES MOVE IN TRENDS

If one cannot accept this premise, there is no point in studying technical analysis. The PremiereTrade trading method was written to help identify trends and their early stages of development for the purpose of trading in agreement with the direction of those trends. We follow trends because trends have shown that once they are in motion, they are most likely to continue rather than reverse.

Over the last hundred years or so, technicians have identified and catalogued chart patterns. They also have worked very hard at creating chart indicators (mathematical formulas) that show weakness or strength of market price. *Research has shown that these patterns and indicators have worked in the past, and therefore when they repeat themselves, they work in the present and future.*

There has been a tendency in the past to discount technical analysis and criticize it, calling it a "self-fulfilling prophecy." Critics claim that because chart patterns have been widely publicized in the last several years, traders are quite familiar with these patterns and therefore act on them in concert, creating bull and bear markets because of bullish and bearish patterns. Critics also claim that patterns are completely subjective and therefore literally in the mind of the beholder.

However, these two criticisms contradict one another. If chart patterns and the positions of chart indicators are completely subjective and in the mind of the beholder, then it is very hard to imagine how everyone could see the same thing at the same time.

The more one studies chart and indicator patterns, the clearer it becomes that reading and interpreting patterns are more an art form than a skill. This admission should not intimidate the prospective technician. Instead, it should be a guiding principle to help the trader to study and learn how to interpret patterns and chart indicators and a reminder that there may be more than meets the eye at first glance.

BAR AND CANDLESTICK CHARTS

Charts come in various different shapes and sizes. PremiereTrade recommends the use of two types of price charts: bar charts and candlestick charts. *Bar charts* (Figure 8-1) display price data in vertical lines, which represent price action during a given time interval. The bar connects the high and low of prices. The tip at the top of the vertical line is the high for that interval, and the tip at the bottom of the vertical line is the low for that interval. The open and close of the bar are displayed by small horizontal dashes called *tics*. The tic to the left of the line is the open, and the tic to the right of the line is the close.

Candlestick charts (Figure 8-2) are similar to bar charts in that the top tip of a vertical line represents the high and the bottom tip represents the low. However, market activity between the open and the close is represented differently by the use of candlestick *bodies*. A hollow body shows a higher closing above a lower opening. A shaded body shows a lower closing below a higher opening. The price activity above and below candlestick bodies is often referred to as *wicks* or *tails*. While the Japanese have used candlestick charts for centuries, they have only recently become popular in the West. Various bullish and bearish candlestick patterns are shown in Figure 8.3*a-s.*

FIGURE 8-1 Bar Charts   **FIGURE 8-2 Candle Stick Charts**

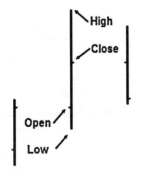

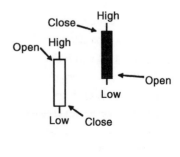

FIGURE 8-3

The **bullish** pattern candle is displayed by a green body. It occurs when prices open near the low prices and close near the period's high price.

(a)

The **bearish** pattern candle is displayed by a red body. It occurs when prices open near the high price and close near the period's low price.

(b)

Hammer - The Hammer is a bullish pattern if it occurs after a significant downtrend. If the line occurs after a significant uptrend, it is called a hanging man. A hammer is identified by a small body and a long wick. The body can be clear, green, or red.

(c)

Hanging Man - This pattern is bearish if it occurs after a significant uptrend. If this pattern occurs after a significant downtrend, it is called a hammer. A hanging man is identified by small candle bodies and a long wick below the bodies.

(d)

Piercing Line - This is a bullish pattern. The first candle is a long bear candle followed by a long bull candle. The bull candle opens lower than the bear's low but closes more than halfway above the middle of the bear candle's body.

(e)

Dark Cloud Cover - This is a bearish pattern. The pattern is more significant if the second candle is below the center of the previous candle's body.

(f)

Bullish Engulfing Line - This pattern is strongly bullish if it occurs after a significant downtrend (it may serve as a reversal pattern). It occurs when a small bearish (red) candle is engulfed by a large bullish (green) candle.

(g)

Bearish Engulfing Line - This pattern is strongly bearish if it occurs after a significant uptrend (it may serve as a reversal pattern). It occurs when a small bullish (green) candle is engulfed by a large bearish (red) candle.

(h)

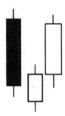 **Morning Star** - This is a bullish pattern signifying a potential bottom. The star indicates a possible reversal and the bullish (green) candle confirms this. The star can be a bullish (green) or a bearish (red) candle.

(i)

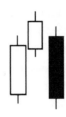 **Evening Star** - This is a bearish pattern signifying a potential top. This indicates a possible reversal and the bearish (red) candle confirms this. The star can be bullish (green) candle or a bearish (red) candle.

(j)

 **Bullish Doji Star** - This star indicates a reversal and a doji indicates indecision. Thus, this pattern usually indicates a reversal following an indecisive period.

(k)

 **Doji Star** - This star indicates a reversal and a doji indicates indecision. Thus, this pattern usually indicates a reversal following an indecisive period. One should wait for a confirmation (like an evening star) before trading a doji star.

(l)

 **Doji** - This candle implies indecision. The open and close are the same.

(m)

 **Shooting Star** - This pattern suggests a minor reversal when it appears after a rally. The star's body must appear near the low price, and the candle should have a long upper wick.

(n)

 Double Doji - This candle (two adjacent doji candle) implies that a forceful move will follow a breakout from the current indecision.

(0)

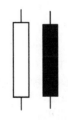 **Spinning Tops** - This is a neutral pattern that occurs when the distance between the high and low and the distance between the open and close are relatively small.

(p)

(Continued)

FIGURE 8-3 *(continued)*

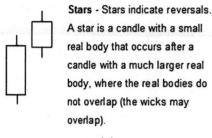

Stars - Stars indicate reversals. A star is a candle with a small real body that occurs after a candle with a much larger real body, where the real bodies do not overlap (the wicks may overlap).

(q)

Dragonfly Doji - This candle also signifies a turning point. It occurs when the open and close are the same and the low is significantly higher than the open, close, and low prices.

(r)

Gravestone Doji - This candle also signifies a turning point. It occurs when the open, close, and low prices are the same and the high is significantly higher than the open, close, and low prices.

(s)

TECHNICAL ANALYSIS TERMS

Chart interval refers to the duration of time that passes between the open and the close of a bar or candlestick. There are chart intervals that start at 1 minute and go up to daily, weekly, and even monthly. While some short-term time intervals are used more often for entry and exit points, others are used for the different trading styles and methods with which a trader feels more comfortable.

A superactive trader may use the 3-, 5-, 10-, and 15-minute chart intervals. A swing or position trader, on the other hand, may use the 30-, 60-, and 180-minute and daily charts to determine a possible trade.

I recommend use of the *daily chart,* the *180-minute chart*, the *60-minute chart,* and the *15-minute chart.* These charts can be used separately as a *one-chart trading system*, or two or more charts can be used in combination.

These charts all measure price activity using Greenwich Mean Time (GMT) or Eastern Standard Time (EST) depending on the software being used. During EST, the difference between GMT and EST is 5 hours. During Eastern Daylight Time (EDT), the difference between GMT and EDT is 4 hours.

THE DAY CHART

The *day chart* shows market data in 24-hour increments. Each closed bar or closed candlestick on the chart represents a "day's worth" of price activity. The day chart is the longest interval chart recommended by PremiereTrade (see Figure 8-4).

THE 180-MINUTE CHART

The *180-minute chart* shows market data in 3-hour increments. Each closed bar or closed candlestick on the chart represents 3 hours of price activity (see Figure 8-5).

THE 30-MINUTE CHART

The *30-minute chart* shows market data in 30-minute increments. Each closed bar or closed candlestick on the chart represents ½ hour of price activity (see Figure 8-6).

THE 15-MINUTE CHART

The *15-minute chart* shows market data in 15-minute increments. Each closed bar or closed candlestick on the chart represents 15 minutes of price activity.

Although I recommend long-term chart intervals, the choice will strictly depend on the trader and his or her comfort with the FOREX to choose time intervals that work best for his or her style of trading. For superactive traders, a 15-minute chart may be the long-term interval, and entry and exits are determined by a 3-minute chart (see Figure 8-7).

I highly recommend that you become very familiar with the FOREX before trading at a superactive level. Money management becomes crucial, and carefully watching the market becomes a necessity.

Figures 8-4 through 8-6 illustrate chart intervals as they appear in different time frames. Notice how market activity becomes increasingly more detailed on the 180- and 60-minute charts compared with the daily chart.

MARKET PATTERNS: UPTRENDS, DOWNTRENDS, AND SIDEWAYS TRENDS

Markets expand and retrace constantly. It is the nature of the market to surge and then pause or retrace. Market prices may continue to expand for some time, either upward or downward. However, at some point they retrace or make corrective moves, and then they may oscillate between a

88

FIGURE 8-4 EUR/USD Daily 2002–2003

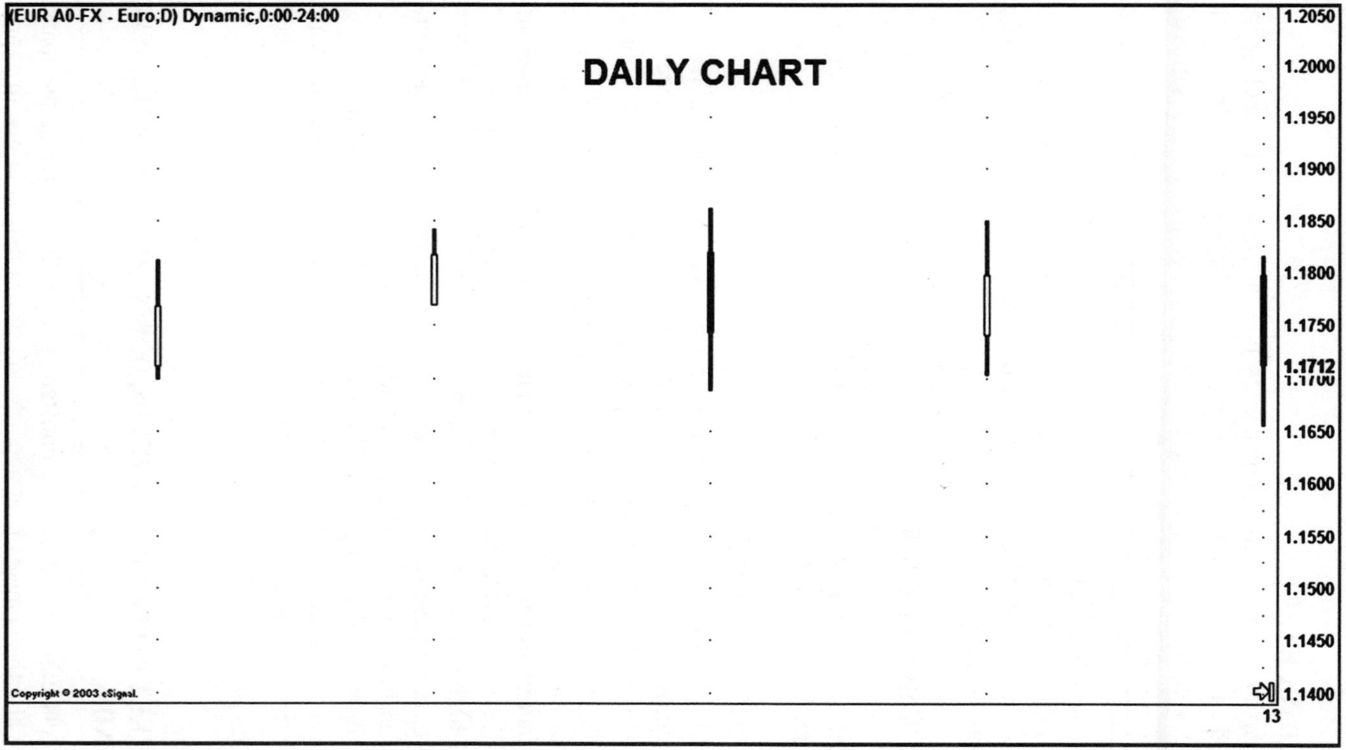

(EUR A0-FX - Euro;D) Dynamic,0:00-24:00

DAILY CHART

| 1.2050 |
| 1.2000 |
| 1.1950 |
| 1.1900 |
| 1.1850 |
| 1.1800 |
| 1.1750 |
| 1.1712 |
| 1.1700 |
| 1.1650 |
| 1.1600 |
| 1.1550 |
| 1.1500 |
| 1.1450 |
| 1.1400 |

13

Copyright © 2003 eSignal.

FIGURE 8-5 EUR/USD 180-Minute 2002–2003

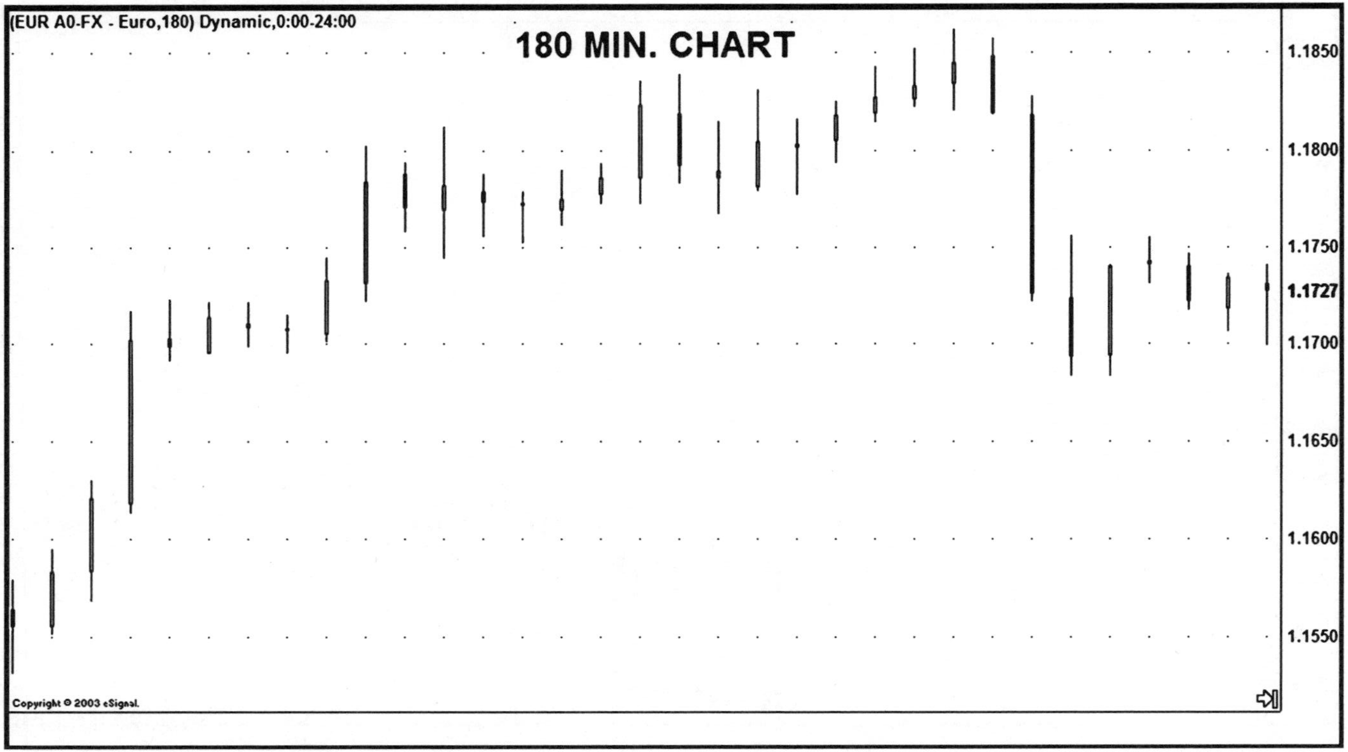

FIGURE 8-6 EUR/USD 60-Minute 2002–2003

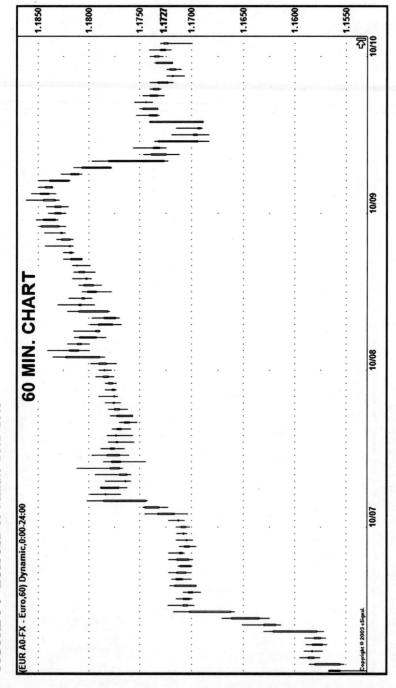

90

distinguishable top and bottom range of prices.

These *retracement moves* are usually between 38 and 62 percent of the previous trend move, which is called a *continuance*. As trends move, they make a series of *peaks* and *troughs* as they move. An *uptrend* consists of a series of ascending peaks and troughs, whereas a *downtrend* consists of descending peaks and troughs. A *sideways trend* consists of horizontal peaks and troughs.

UPTREND/UPSWING

An *uptrend* is a market consisting of price patterns of higher highs (peaks) and higher lows (troughs) in which buying pressure is the dominant force (see Figure 8-7).

DOWNTREND/DOWNSWING

A *downtrend* is a market consisting of price patterns of lower lows (troughs) and lower highs (peaks) in which selling pressure is the dominant force (see Figure 8-8).

SIDEWAYS AND CHANNEL TRENDS

As we study chart patterns, one comes to mind that might be the easiest to understand—channel patterns. A *channel pattern* generally should be considered to be a continuation pattern.

Channel patterns are typically consolidation areas that usually are a midpoint of the move in the direction of the trend. Research has shown that these patterns are generally 3 to 6 months long and vary on the short-term and minute time frames. However, they can be much longer.

The trendlines run parallel in a rectangle. Supply and demand seems evenly balanced within the pattern, whereas buyers and sellers are equally matched each time the currency pair reaches one of the rectangle trendlines. The same highs are constantly tested, as are the same lows.

As the currency pair vacillates between these two clearly set support and resistance levels, you can trade long and short at each junction. Your stop loss or cover point would be just beyond one of the trendlines.

Volume isn't as important as in other patterns, but there usually is a lessening of activity within the pattern. As in the other patterns, though, volume should increase noticeably on the breakout (see Figure 8-9).

Since these movements oscillate between a *range* of prices, we also call *wide* sideways trends *ranger markets*. Generally speaking, we avoid trading in *narrow* sideways trends. Sideways trends are simply when the price of the position moves sideways. I will use the same example. A

FIGURE 8-7 EUR/USD Daily 2002–2003

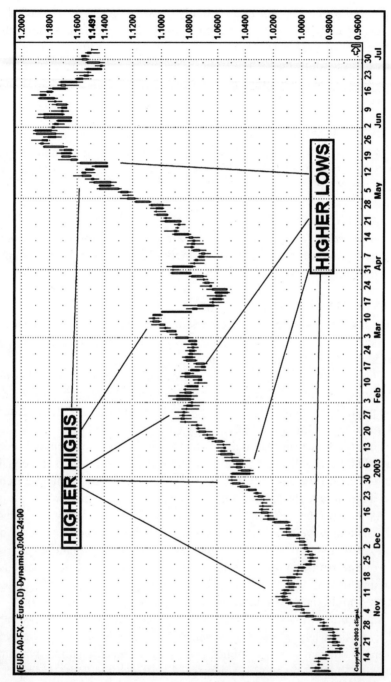

FIGURE 8-8   CHF/USD Daily 2002–2003

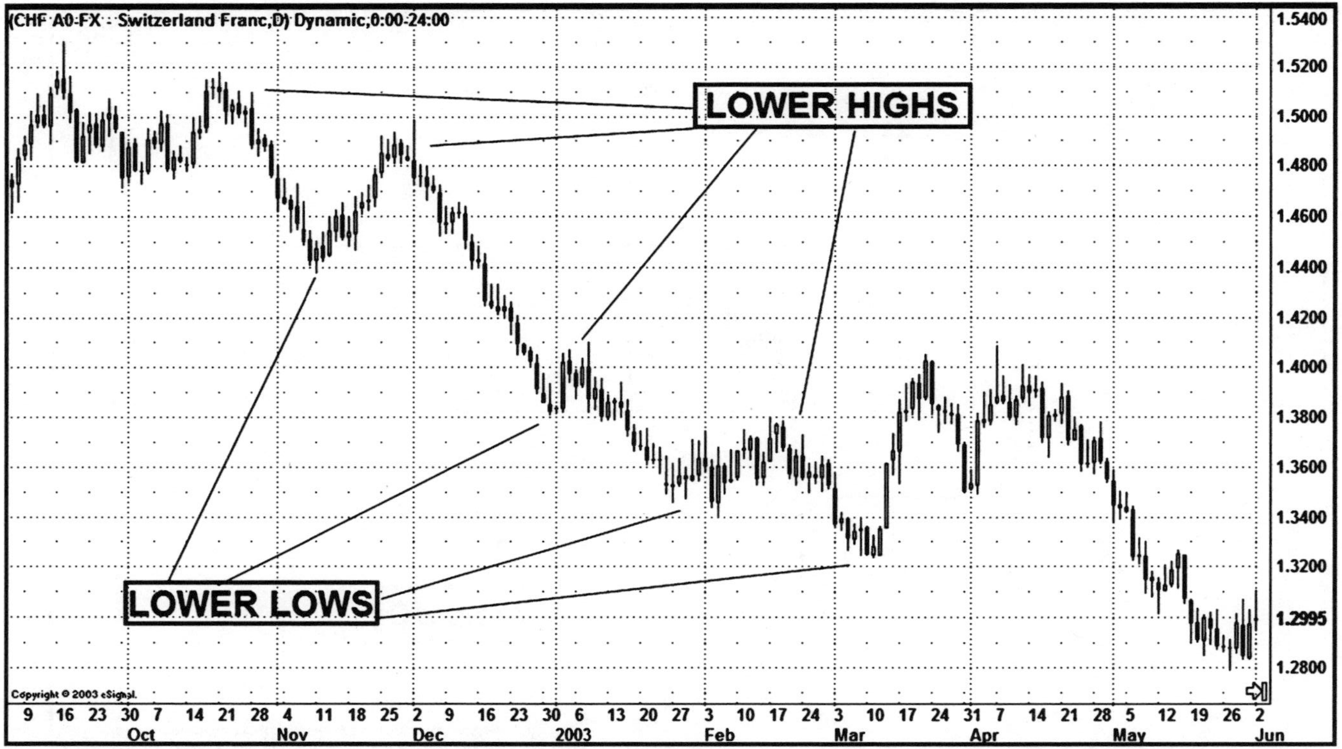

FIGURE 8-9 GBP/USD Daily 2002–2003

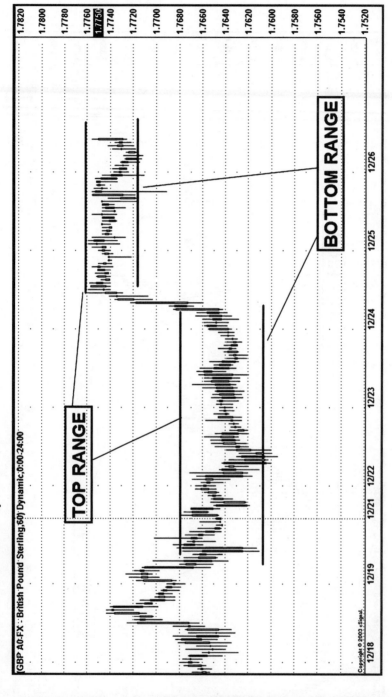

position say trades at 10 dollars and then goes to 12 dollars, and then continues to move between 10 and 12 dollars. The position goes to 12 dollars and then back to 10 dollars, this is moving sideways or a channel.

In Figure 8-10 and 8-11, compare and contrast the difference between up/down trends and sideways trends.

SUPPORT AND RESISTANCE

As mentioned earlier, trends consist of ascending, descending, or horizontal peaks and troughs. Let's now give those peaks and troughs their appropriate names and introduce the concepts of support and resistance. The troughs, or reaction lows, in an uptrend are called *support*. The peaks, or reaction highs, in a downtrend are called *resistance*.

Support and resistance (S&R) constitute one of the oldest technical analysis principles. S&R is like a "tug of war" between buyers and sellers. Support levels are prices at which sellers are unwilling to accept lower prices and buying pressure exceeds selling pressure. Resistance levels are prices at which buyers are unwilling to pay higher prices and selling pressure exceeds buying pressure.

S&R principles include

- *Major support* is the bottom range of prices.

- *Major resistance* is the top range of prices.

- *Intermediate support and resistance* is a price level where the market tends to stall, reverse, pause, or continue between major support and major resistance (see Figure 8-12).

- When a resistance level is broken successfully, it often becomes support.

- When a support level is broken successfully, it often becomes resistance (see Figure 8-13).

MOVING AVERAGES

A *moving average* is an indicator that shows the average price of a currency over a period of time. As prices change enough to affect the average, the indicator line moves up or down in an attempt to depict the more meaningful price changes and reduces the depiction of the less meaningful price activity.

FIGURE 8-10 EUR/USD Daily 2002–2003

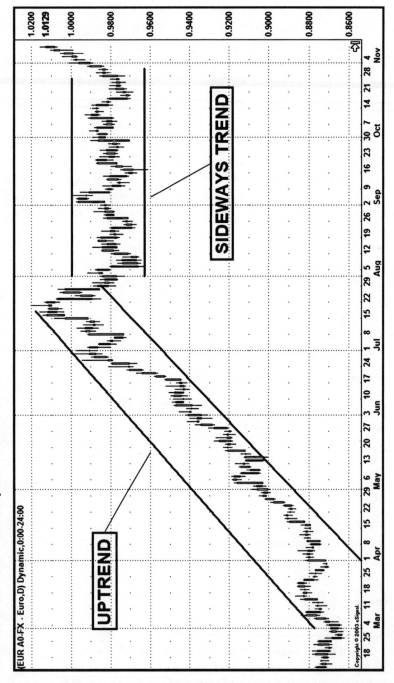

FIGURE 8-11 CHF/USD Daily 2002–2003

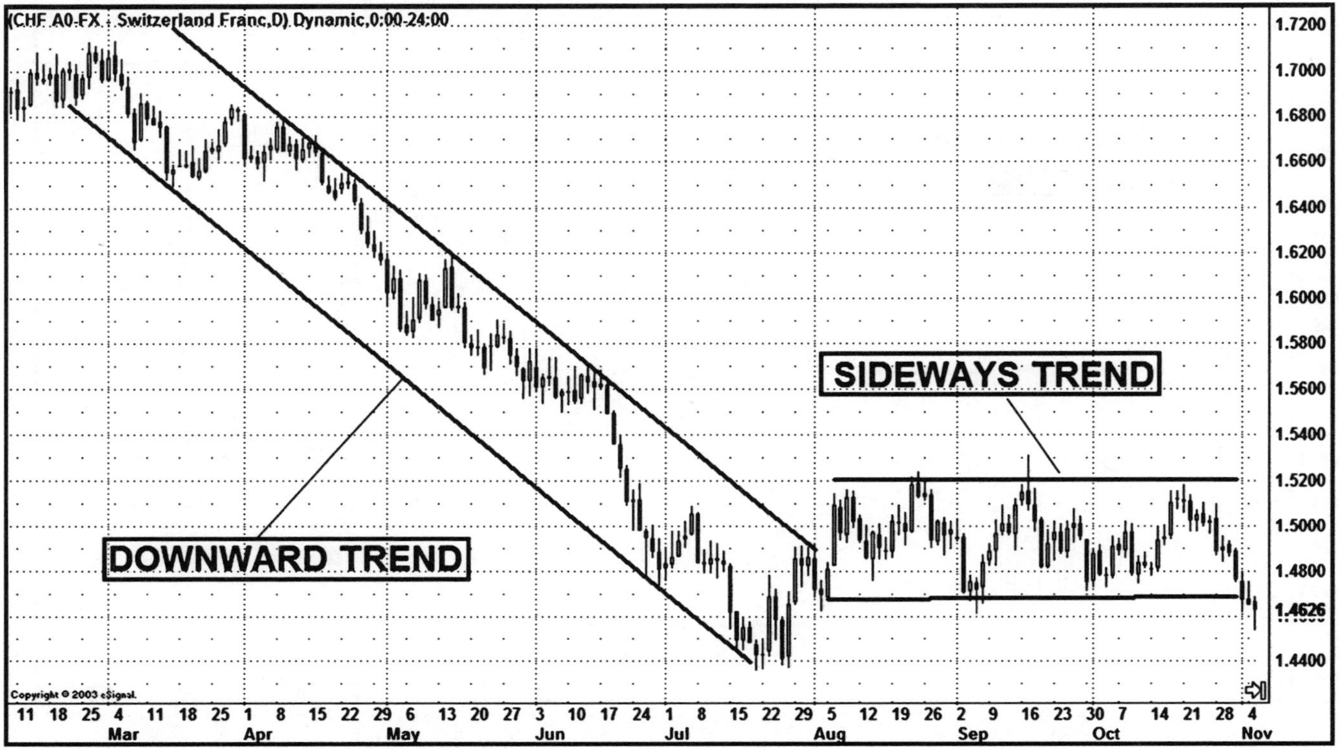

(CHF, A0-FX ; Switzerland Franc,D) Dynamic,0:00-24:00

SIDEWAYS TREND

DOWNWARD TREND

Copyright © 2003 eSignal.

FIGURE 8-12 GBP/USD Daily 2002–2003

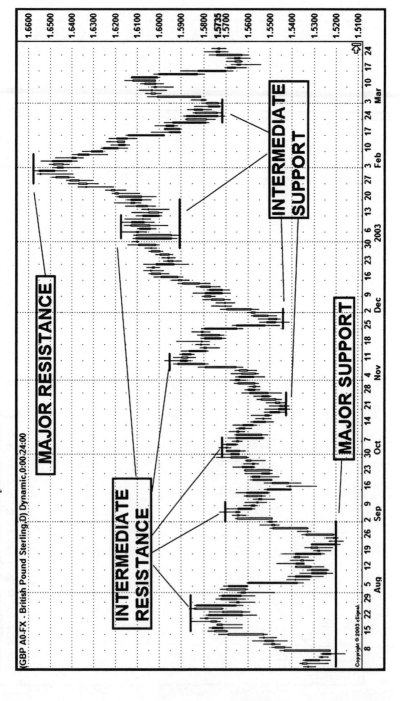

FIGURE 8-13 GBP/USD Daily 2002–2003

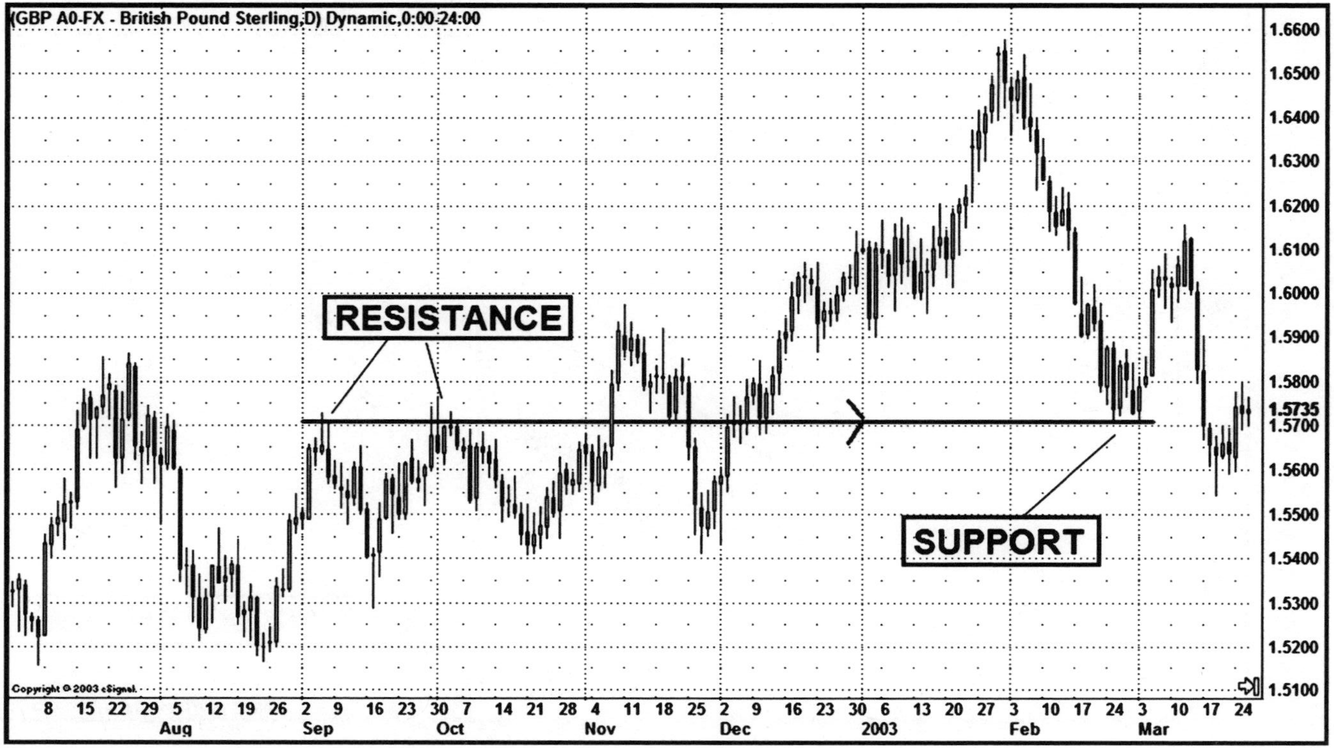

(GBP A0-FX - British Pound Sterling;D) Dynamic,0:00-24:00

RESISTANCE

SUPPORT

1.6600
1.6500
1.6400
1.6300
1.6200
1.6100
1.6000
1.5900
1.5800
1.5735
1.5700
1.5600
1.5500
1.5400
1.5300
1.5200
1.5100

8 15 22 29 5 12 19 26 2 9 16 23 30 7 14 21 28 4 11 18 25 2 9 16 23 30 6 13 20 27 3 10 17 24 3 10 17 24
Aug   Sep   Oct   Nov   Dec   2003   Feb   Mar

Copyright © 2003 eSignal.

99

FIGURE 8-14 EUR/USD Daily 2002–2003

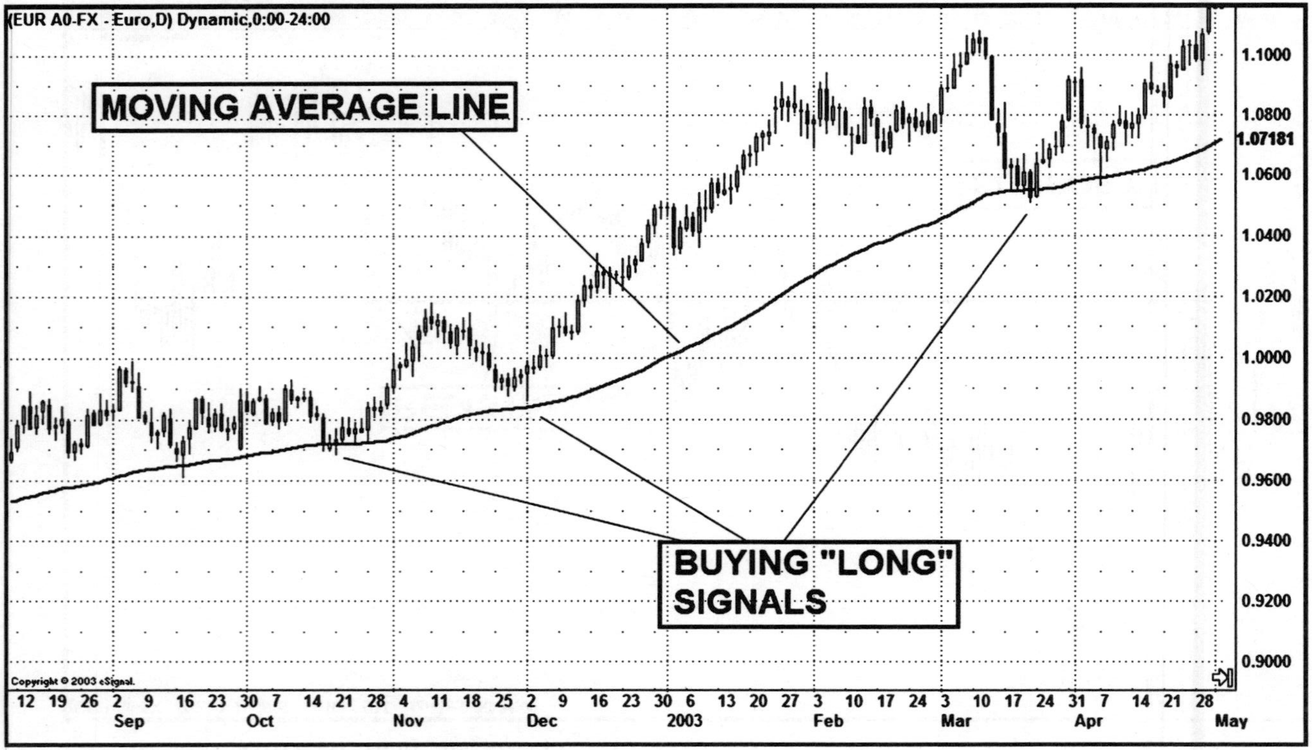

(EUR A0-FX - Euro,D) Dynamic,0:00-24:00

MOVING AVERAGE LINE

BUYING "LONG" SIGNALS

Copyright © 2003 eSignal.

1.1000
1.0800
1.07181
1.0600
1.0400
1.0200
1.0000
0.9800
0.9600
0.9400
0.9200
0.9000

12 19 26 2 9 16 23 30 7 14 21 28 4 11 18 25 2 9 16 23 30 6 13 20 27 3 10 17 24 3 10 17 24 31 7 14 21 28
Sep   Oct   Nov   Dec   2003 Feb   Mar   Apr   May

There are five popular types of moving averages: simple (also referred to as *arithmetic*), exponential, triangular, variable, and weighted. Moving averages can be calculated on any data series, including an open, high, low, close, or another indicator.

The only significant difference between the various types of moving averages is the weight assigned to the most recent data. Simple moving averages apply equal weight to the prices. Exponential and weighted averages apply more weight to recent prices. The most popular method of interpreting a moving average is to compare the relationship between a moving average of price with the price itself.

A moving average is often used to identify the trend of a market. It can be used in conjunction with other averages to generate buy and sell signals when the averages cross. Moving averages of all types also can be used as a filter within a trading system to reduce *whipsaws*. For example, you may only want to take long trades when the average is moving in an upward direction or when price is above the moving average.

Generally speaking, a *buy signal* is generated when price opens and closes *above* its moving average. This indicates that support has established itself as the dominant force. Conversely, a *sell signal* is generated when the price opens and closes *below* its moving average, indicating that resistance has established itself as the dominant force.

In strong vector trends, a moving average can act as a "price floor" in an uptrend and as a "price ceiling" in a downtrend. In sideways trends or ranger markets, the moving average acts as a moving-average midpoint (see Figure 8-14).

As this chapter has shown, technical analysis is a great way to help your trading efforts and is probably the most widely used tool in trading. You need to find the right technical tool for your trading style.

You probably have come across software that takes this information into account and does the work for you. This is okay. Just remember that you are looking for a way to trade the same way every time. Take the emotion out and place your entry and exits the exact same way every time. That is what the professionals do.

9

ADVANCED TRADING CHARTS AND INDICATORS

- Tools for Technical Analysis
- Bollinger Bands
- Directional Movement Index (DMI)
- Stochastic Indicator
- Moving Averages (Simple, Weighted, and Exponential)
- Moving Average Convergence/Divergence (MAC/D)
- Momentum
- Relative Strength Indicator (RSI)
- Rate of Change (ROC)
- Volume

TOOLS FOR TECHNICAL ANALYSIS

Each chart and indicator plays a unique role in the overall analysis process. Observe how each indicator in Figure 9-1 depicts trending and nontrending conditions. The *intervals* (time periods) and *indicators* (studies) are useful in spotting interday or intraday turning points caused by large moves, retracements, continuances, and reversals.

The goal is to observe how each indicator shows direction, entry, exit, or weakness or strength of markets in trending or nontrending conditions. Each indicator performs differently in both trending markets and nontrending markets, and therefore, these differences must be noticed, memorized, and catalogued to make the best use of these tools.

BOLLINGER BANDS

> *What are Bollinger bands?* They are curves drawn in and around the price structure that provide relative definitions of high and low.
>
> *What are Bollinger bands used for?* Knowing whether prices are high or low, the investor/trader can make rational investment decisions by comparing price action with the actions of indicators.
>
> *What can Bollinger bands be applied to?* Most anything—currency pairs, indices, futures, and mutual funds.
>
> *How are Bollinger bands calculated?* The base for a band is a moving average, and the band's width is determined by volatility (see Figure 9-2).

John Bollinger is a giant in today's trading community. His Bollinger Bands sharpen the sensitivity of fixed indicators, allowing them to more precisely reflect a market's volatility. By more accurately indicating the existing market environment, they are seen by many as today's standard—and most reliable—tool for plotting expected price action.

Mr. John Bollinger notes the following characteristics of Bollinger bands:

- Sharp price changes tend to occur after the bands tighten and as volatility lessens.

- When prices move outside the bands, a continuation of the current trend is implied.

- Bottoms and tops made outside the bands followed by bottoms and tops made inside the bands call for reversals in the trend.

FIGURE 9-1 EUR/USD Daily Chart 2002–2003

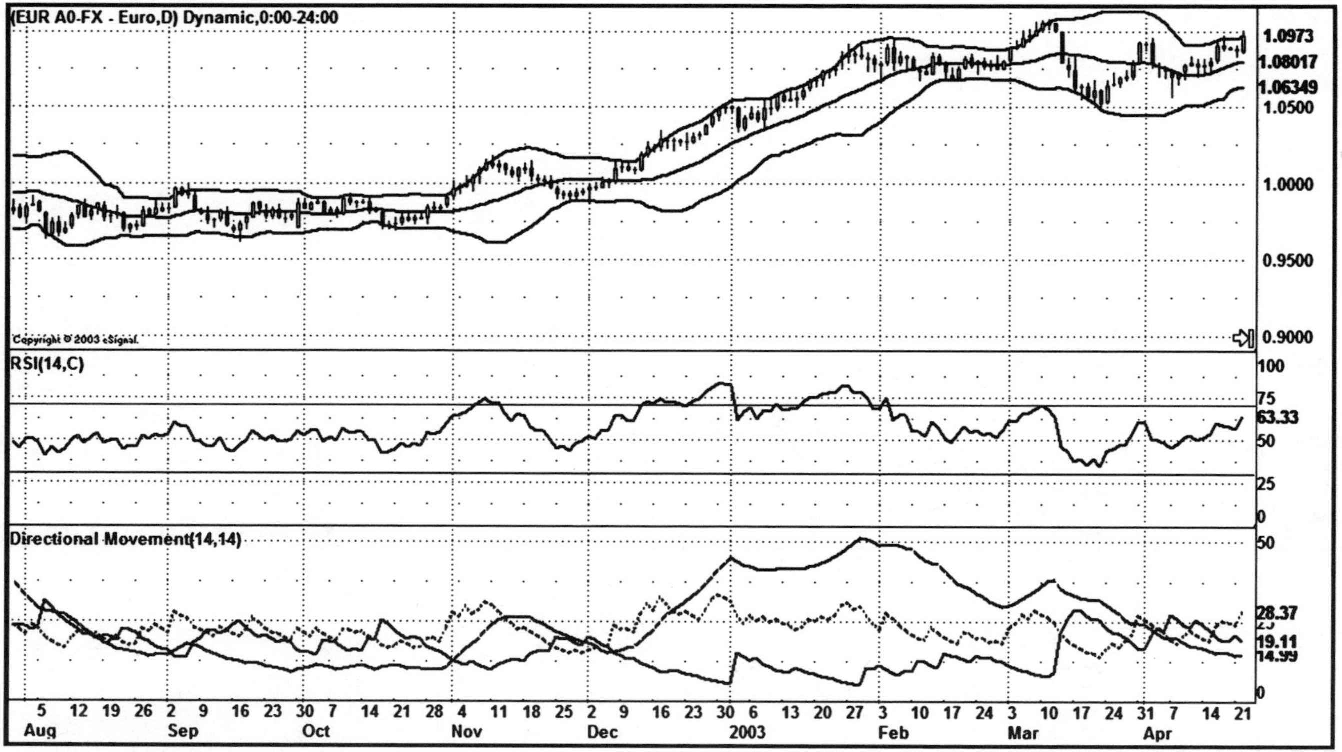

105

FIGURE 9-2   Bollinger Bands

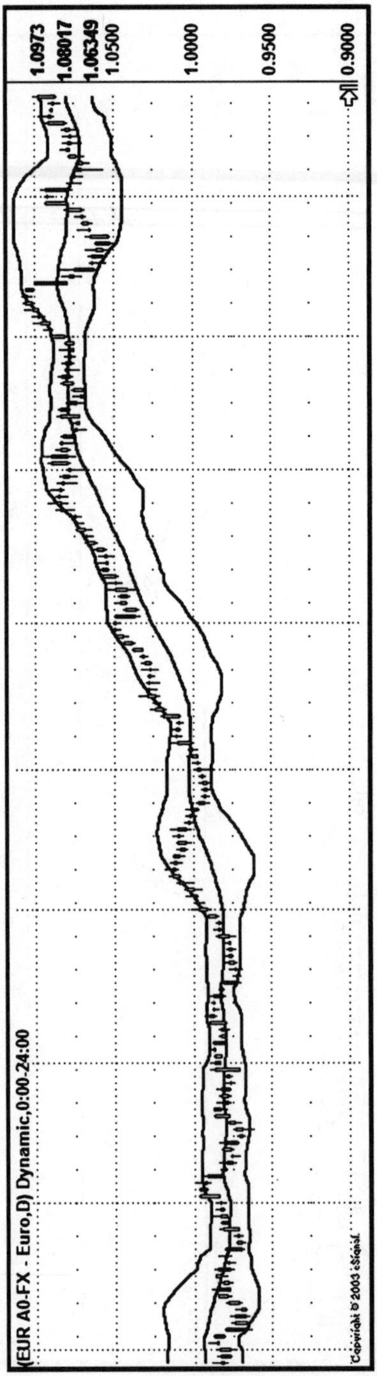

106

- A move that originates at one band tends to go all the way to the other band. (This observation is useful when projecting price targets.)

Bollinger bands are plotted at standard deviation levels above and below a moving average. Since standard deviation is a measure of volatility, the bands are self-adjusting—widening during volatile markets and contracting during calmer periods. The bands bracket approximately 90 percent of the market activity.

The 10 percent outside the bands is most likely going to approximate areas where prices will return to within the bands. When the bands are flat and narrow, this indicates that price volatility is lower than in previous time periods.

When the bands begin to flare, this indicates increased volatility and the possible inception of a new, strong directional or trend move. Wide bands are an indication of a very strong move.

DIRECTIONAL MOVEMENT INDEX (DMI)

Developed by Welles Wilder, the DMI consists of two indicators: the average directional index (ADX) and the directional index (DI), which is both positive and negative (DI+ and DI−). Figure 9-3 illustrates the DMI.

The ADX measures the *strength* of a prevailing trend, rising when the direction is strong and falling when the prior confirmed trend or direction is weakening. The ADX is *not a directional* indicator. ADX attempts to measure the trending quality of the market, isolating those periods where the market is not trending.

DI+ and DI− show *direction*. When DI+ rises above DI−, upward direction is confirmed. When DI− rises above DI+, downward direction is confirmed. When the move is strong, ADX is rising and DI+ and DI− remain apart.

STOCHASTIC INDICATOR

The stochastic indicator identifies swings, tops, and bottoms. Popularized by Dr. George C. Lane of Investment Educators, the stochastic indicator measures the position of a currency pair compared with its most recent trading range (see Figure 9-4).

You may have heard the stochastic indicator referred to as the "overbought" or "oversold" indicator. Specifically, it measures the relationship between the closing price of a currency pair and its high and low during a specific number of days or weeks.

FIGURE 9-3 Directional Movement Index (DMI)

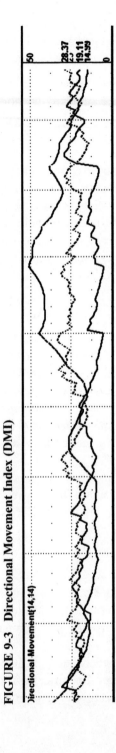

FIGURE 9-4 Stochastic Indicator

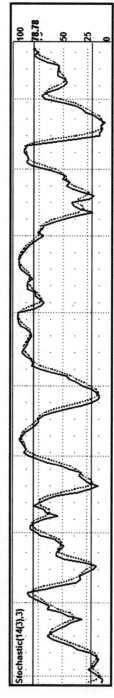

As the price of a currency pair rises, the closing price tends to be, on average, closer and closer to the extreme highs of the currency pair, and as prices fall, the closing price tends to fall, on average, closer and closer to the extreme lows. This indicator tries to find a correlation between the moving closing price of a currency pair and its reversal tendencies. It does a wonderful job and is used widely by most traders.

Stochastic indicator points out overbought and oversold conditions and is considered a highly accurate method for picking tops and bottoms. The stochastic indicator can be very useful as a timing aid in knowing when to take action in a currency pair, particularly when it is used in conjunction with other technical indicators. The stochastic indicator also may be used with industry groups or market indexes.

MOVING AVERAGES (SIMPLE, WEIGHTED, AND EXPONENTIAL)

Moving averages are a very popular tool among traders because they are a lagging indicator of price swings. Short- and long-term trends are easier to identify. The averages are calculated on the user's specifications and can be formatted to different styles of trading and time frames.

For example, if you use an 89-time-frame moving average, the prices of the last 89 time frames are added together and then divided by 89. As the newest time frame ends, which appears at the end of the average line, the first one gets dropped, and the average line makes an upward, downward, or sideways move.

Along with the different time frames a trader can use, the averages can be calculated based on the opening, high, low, or closing price. You also can use the midpoint of the time frame, which is an average within itself. However, most traders prefer to use the closing price because it is the most important.

There are three different types of moving averages:

1.   The simple moving average
2.   The weighted moving average
3.   The exponentially smoothed moving average

SIMPLE MOVING AVERAGE

A *simple moving average* is just what it says: The prices within time frames are added and then divided by the number of time frames. For example, if you use a daily time frame chart and you are calculating a 10-day moving average, the most current day is added to the moving average and the last day is dropped.

If the price is higher and moves the average higher than the preceding time frame, the moving-average line will start moving upward and show an upward trend. Figure 9-5 provides an example of a 10- and 25-day moving-average chart.

FIGURE 9-5 Simple Moving Average

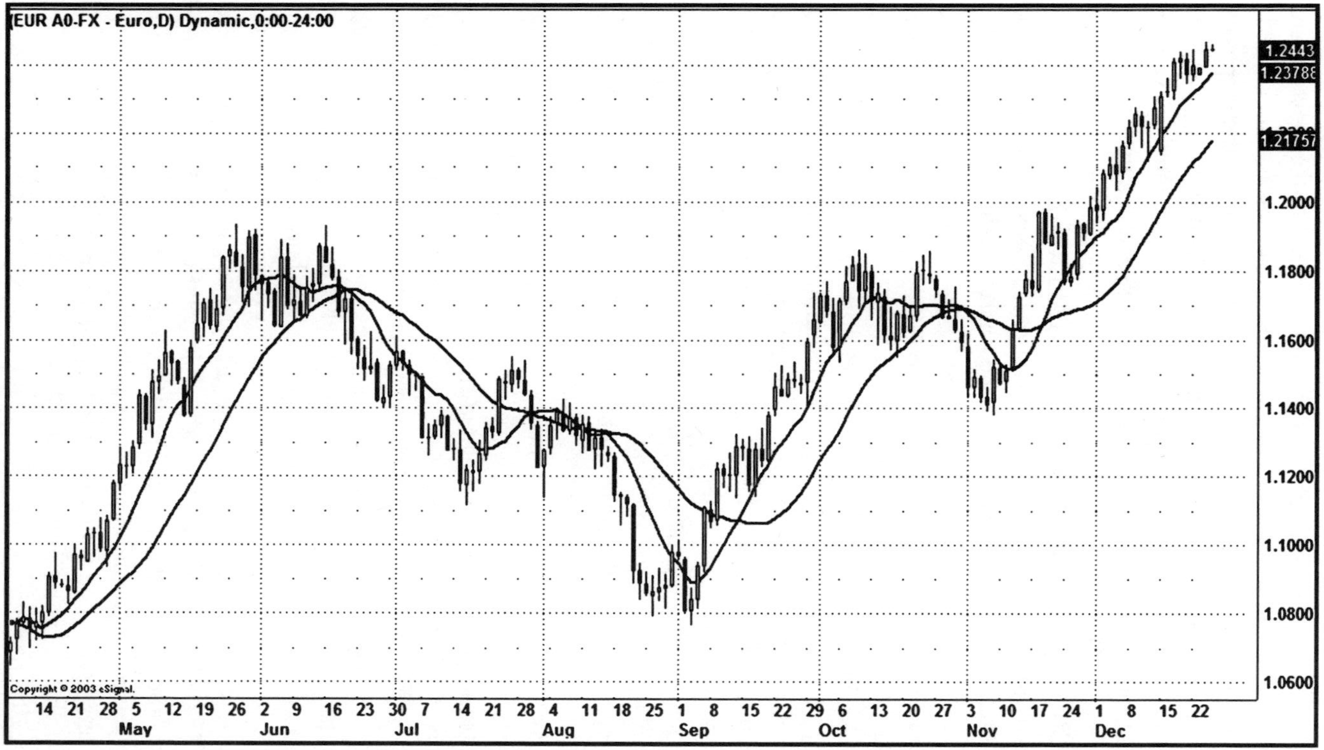

EUR A0.FX - Euro,D) Dynamic,0:00-24:00

1.2443
1.23788
1.21757
1.2000
1.1800
1.1600
1.1400
1.1200
1.1000
1.0800
1.0600

Copyright © 2003 eSignal.

14 21 28 5   12 19 26 2 9   16 23 30 7   14 21 28 4   11 18 25 1 8   15 22 29 6   13 20 27 3   10 17 24 1 8   15 22
May   Jun   Jul   Aug   Sep   Oct   Nov   Dec

111

WEIGHTED MOVING AVERAGE

A *weighted moving average* consigns more weight to the most recent closing prices. Most traders argue that a weighted moving average is used more often on long-term charts because the recent prices get more emphasis, and not as much attention is given to the last few time frames, which are still part of the moving average. Figure 9-6 presents two moving average lines that compare a simple and a weighted moving average line.

EXPONENTIALLY SMOOTHED MOVING AVERAGE

The advantage of an *exponentially smoothed moving average,* unlike the weighted moving average, is that the chart is calculated gradually with less emphasis on prices in later time frames, and the last time frame is dropped. Exponentially smoothed averages assign different weights to the previous prices.

The further down the line the price is located, the less weight is assigned to it. Figure 9-7 provides an example of a 25-day moving-average chart in which the solid line represents a simple moving average, the dotted line represents a weighted moving average, and the dashed line represents an exponentially smoothed moving average.

Generally, you should use only two or three moving averages at one time. You will need to experiment with time frames and the type of average that works best for the currency being traded. An advantage of using moving averages is the ability to back trade.

Back trading is when you take a strategy such as a moving average and look at a price chart. You then work backwards looking at the chart to see how many times you would have entered and exited a trade using your strategy on past performance. There are a lot of software programs out there that will allow you to back test your trading strategies. This is a very effective way to see what might have happened using your respective trading strategy. Just remember that past performance may not always represent future success.

By adding the moving averages, you can see how they have forecasted past trends, reversals, and entry or exit signals. By observing a shorter-term moving average across a longer-term average, a buy or sell signal can be identified.

To avoid fake signals, it is advisable that the longer-term moving average is moving in the same direction as the short-term moving average. Another way to avoid fake signals is to use two moving averages for buy and sell signals and another one for long-term trends.

If you feel comfortable using 10- and 25-day moving averages for entry and exits, perhaps an 89-day moving average, which is much respected among traders, should be used for a long-term trend. Figure 9-8 provides an example of a 10-, 25-, and 89-day moving-average chart.

FIGURE 9-6 Weighted Moving Average

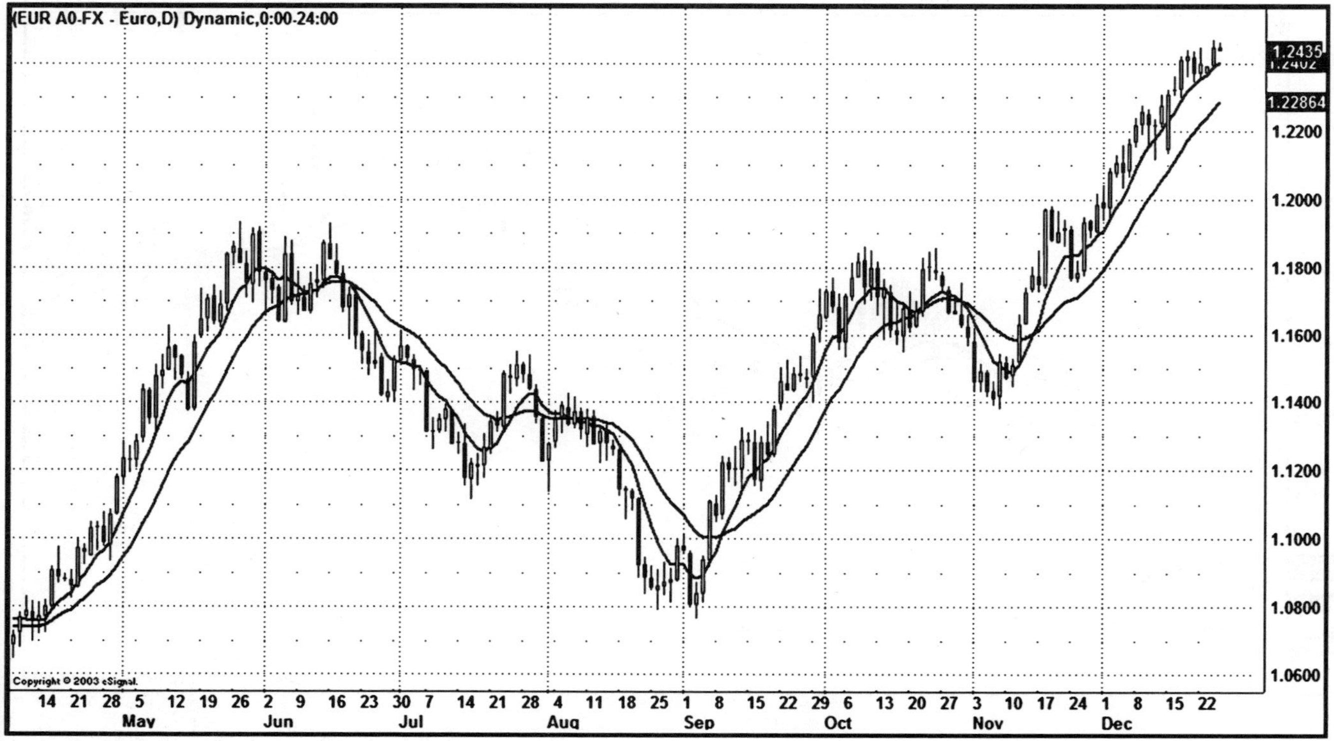

FIGURE 9-7　Moving Average Lines

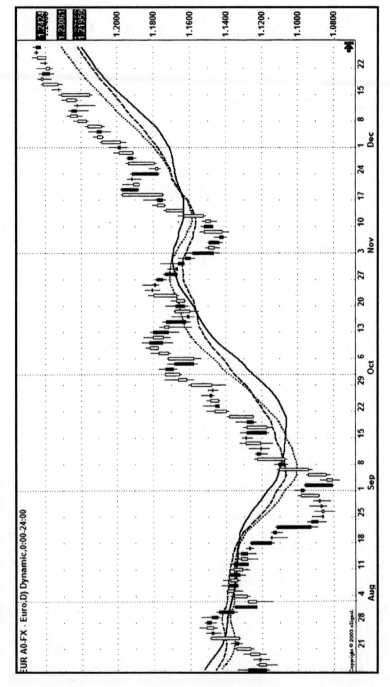

114

FIGURE 9-8 10-, 25-, 89-Day Moving Average Lines

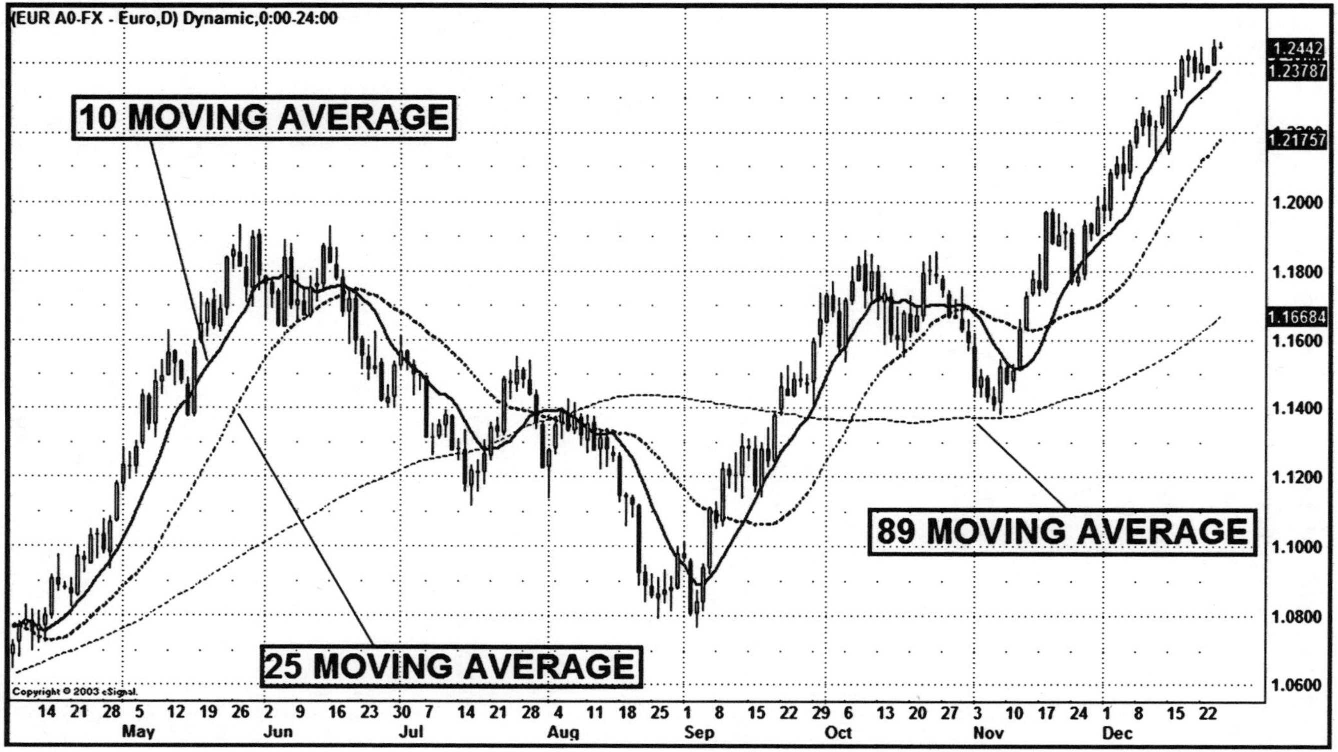

ENTERING A POSITION USING MOVING AVERAGES:

Figure 9-9 shows how to use 10- and 25-day exponential moving averages for buy and sell signals with an 89-day moving average for long-term confirmation.

By using the cross of a shorter-time-frame moving average over a longer-time-frame moving average, we are able to see a trend develop that could be very profitable. It is important to enter these trends at the cross only when the long-term moving average confirms the trend.

In this case, we are using an 89-day moving average as our confirmation line by only entering a long trade (buy) when the cross occurs above the line and a short trade (sell) below the confirmation line.

The captions in Figure 9-9 point out the crosses between the 10- and 25-day moving averages and point out entry points.

The lag and possible sharp trend reversal could result in the loss of a lot of profitable pips. The number of pips you allow your trade to recycle before closing out your trade largely will depend on your trading style and the characteristics of the currency pair you are trading. Using good money management will limit your risk and secure profits, always use stops and limits.

MOVING AVERAGE CONVERGENCE/DIVERGENCE (MAC/D)

The MAC/D is the difference between a 26- and a 12-day exponential moving average. A 9-day exponential moving average, called the *signal* (or *trigger*) *line,* is plotted on top of the MAC/D to show buy/sell opportunities (see Figure 9-10).

The MAC/D proves most effective in wide-swinging trading markets. There are three popular ways to use the MAC/D: crossover, overbought/oversold conditions, and divergences.

The basic MAC/D trading rule is to sell when the MAC/D falls below its signal line. Similarly, a buy signal occurs when the MAC/D rises above its signal line. It is also popular to buy/sell when the MAC/D goes above or below zero.

The MAC/D is also useful as an overbought/oversold indicator. When the shorter moving average pulls away dramatically from the longer moving average (the MAC/D rises), it is likely that the price is overextending and will soon return to more realistic levels. MAC/D overbought and oversold conditions vary from currency pair to currency pair.

FIGURE 9-9 Moving Average Lines with Buy and Sell Signals

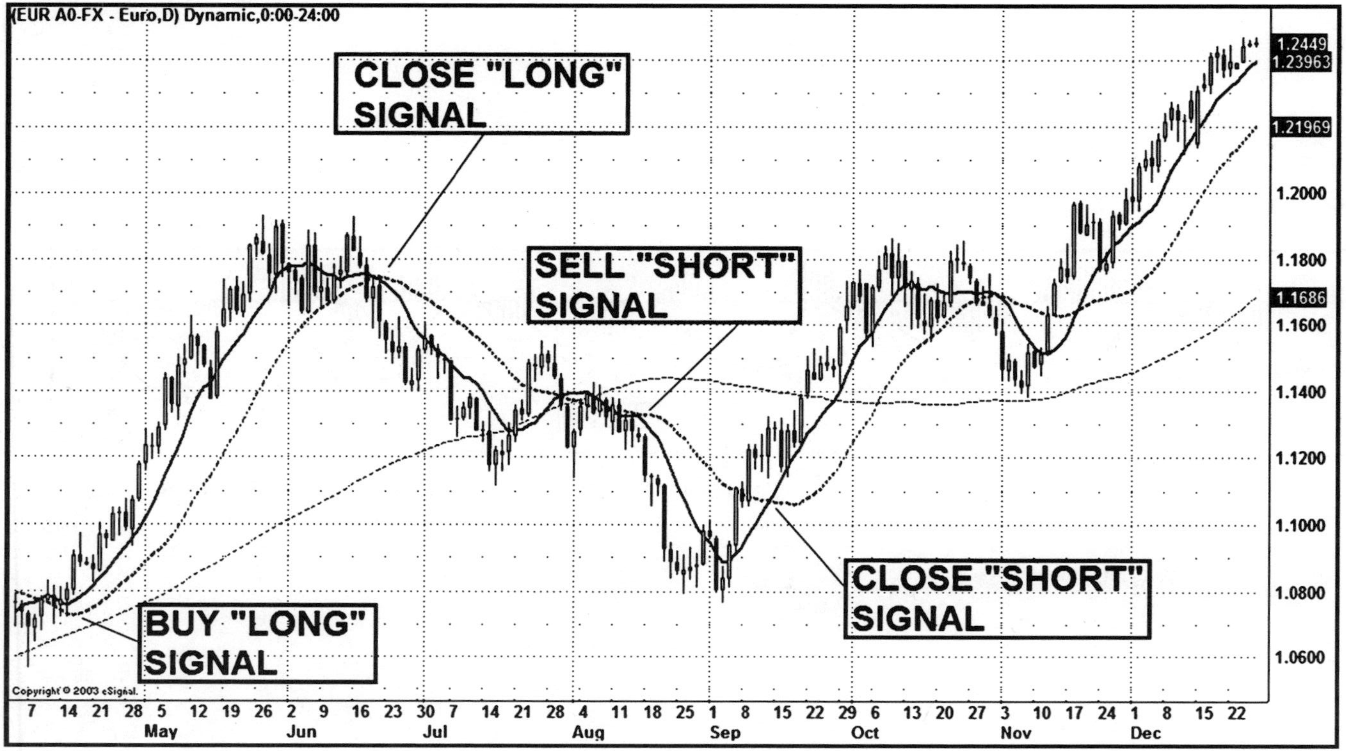

(EUR A0-FX - Euro,D) Dynamic,0:00-24:00

Copyright © 2003 eSignal.

CLOSE "LONG" SIGNAL

SELL "SHORT" SIGNAL

CLOSE "SHORT" SIGNAL

BUY "LONG" SIGNAL

1.2449
1.23963
1.21969
1.2000
1.1800
1.16686
1.1600
1.1400
1.1200
1.1000
1.0800
1.0600

7 14 21 28 5 12 19 26 2 9 16 23 30 7 14 21 28 4 11 18 25 1 8 15 22 29 6 13 20 27 3 10 17 24 1 8 15 22
May   Jun   Jul   Aug   Sep   Oct   Nov   Dec

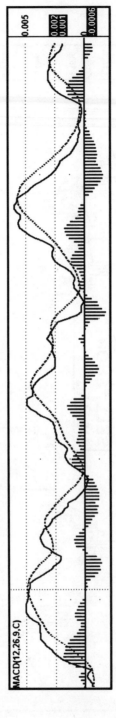

FIGURE 9-10   Moving Average Convergence/Divergence (MACD)

An indication that an end to the current trend may be near occurs when the MAC/D diverges from the currency pair. A bearish divergence occurs when the MAC/D is making new lows and the prices fail to reach those new lows. A bullish divergence occurs when the MAC/D is making new highs and the prices fail to reach those new highs. Both these divergences are most significant when they occur at relatively overbought/oversold levels.

MOMENTUM

Momentum is an oscillator designed to measure the rate of price change, not the actual price level. This oscillator consists of the net difference between the current closing price and the oldest closing price from a pre-determined period (see Figure 9-11).

In terms of time, the shorter the number of days included in the calculations, the more responsive the momentum will be to short-term fluctuations, and vice versa. The signal triggered by the crossing of the zero line remains in effect. However, such signals should be followed only when they are consistent with the ongoing trend.

RELATIVE STRENGTH INDEX (RSI)

The relative strength index (RSI) is designed to indicate a market's current strength or weakness, depending on where prices close during a given period. It is based on the premise that higher closes indicate strong markets and lower closes indicate weak markets (see Figure 9-12).

The RSI is plotted on a 0 to 100 scale. Generally, a buy signal is generated when the RSI moves up through the lower band (band set to 30), and a sell signal is generated when the RSI moves down through the upper band (band set to 70).

The buy and sell levels will vary somewhat depending on the length you choose for the RSI calculation. Once you are in a position, a warning signal to close that position is indicated by values above 85, which indicate an overbought condition (selling signal), and values under 15, which indicate an oversold condition (buying signal).

A shorter length time frame will result in the RSI being more volatile. A longer length time frame results in a less volatile RSI, which reaches extremes far less often. Different uses will result in slightly different levels at which the price changes direction.

FIGURE 9-11 Momentum

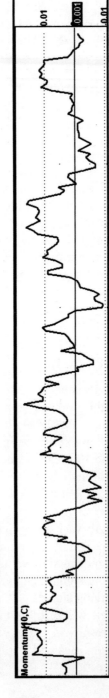

FIGURE 9-12   Relative Strength Index (RSI)

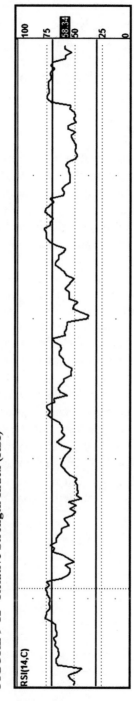

The band levels are usually close to each other. Most prices seem to change direction at 30 and 70. It is important to note that this is not a hard-and-fast rule, and I recommend playing with the band levels until you find the best one for the issue you are looking at.

RATE OF CHANGE (ROC)

ROC is another version of the momentum oscillator. The difference lies in the formula. While the momentum oscillator's formula is based on sub-tracting the oldest closing price from the most recent closing price, the ROC formula is based on dividing the oldest closing price into the most recent closing price. Looking at both graphs for the same currency pair and price period shows very little difference (see Figure 9-13).

VOLUME

The volume indicator is used to show the strength of an up or down move-ment. A movement accompanied by increasing volume is likely to continue with more strength than one accompanied by decreasing volume (see Fig-ure 9-14).

While many professionals use the volume indicator as their only tool in trading, others use it in conjunctions with price charts, economic news, and geopolitical news. The volume indicator is a great source for confirmation, entry and exit signals, and overall decision making.

You will find a few of the indicators discussed in this chapter with which you will feel comfortable, and you will learn to discern trends on different currencies and time intervals that will help you to become a better trader.

FIGURE 9-13   Rate of Change (ROC)

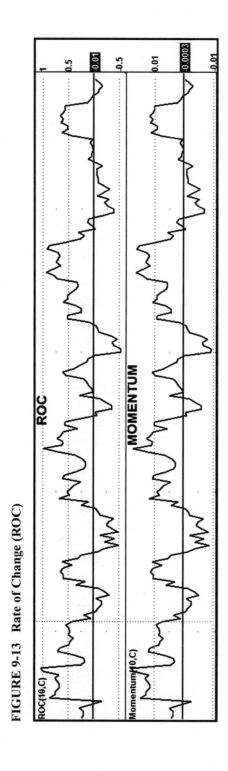

FIGURE 9-14 Volume

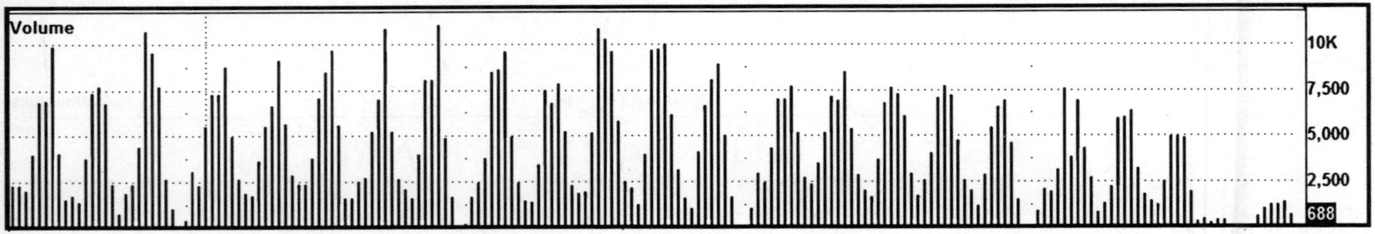

10

FIBONACCI NUMERICAL SEQUENCES AND ELLIOT WAVES

- Introduction
- Fibonacci Rectangles and Shell Spirals
- Fibonacci Retracements
- Fibonacci Extensions
- Fibonacci Time
- Fibonacci Circles
- Elliot Waves

INTRODUCTION

Leonardo Fibonacci, a mathematician in the 1200s, created a numerical sequence of numbers. From left to right after the first two numbers, the values increase successively, and each number, in turn, is determined by the sum of the previous two numbers. For example, in the Fibonacci sequence 1, 1, 2, 3, 5, 8, 13, 21, 34, 55, 89, 144, 233, 377, to get the next number in the series after 377, add 233 to 377 and arrive at 610.

Many technicians use Fibonacci sequences in their technical analyses when attempting to determine support and resistance, and they commonly use 38.2, 50, and 61.8 percent retracements. It is commonly thought that a 0.382 retracement from a trend tends to imply a continuation of the trend. A 0.618 retracement implies that a trend change may be in the making. Technicians have adopted many such rules.

It is easier to see what is happening if we plot the ratios on a graph (see Figure 10-1). As the figure shows, the ratio seems to be settling down to a particular value. We call this value the *golden ratio* or the *golden number.* It has a value of approximately 1.61804.

The other interesting relationship of this number sequence is that if we take the ratio of two successive numbers in the Fibonacci series (i.e., we divide each number by the number after it in the sequence), we will move toward a particular constant value. This value is 0.6180345, which has been referred to as the *golden ratio.*

FIGURE 10-1 Fibonacci Graph

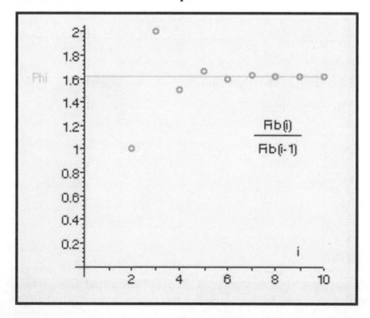

If you also calculate the ratios using alternate numbers in the Fibonacci series (i.e., do the same calculation but skip over a number), the resulting ratio approaches 0.38196.

FIBONACCI RECTANGLES AND SHELL SPIRALS

We can make a picture showing the Fibonacci sequence 1, 1, 2, 3, 5, 8, 13, 21 if we start with two small squares of size 1 next to each other. On top of both these small square, draw a square of size 2 (= 1 + 1). Now draw a new square—touching both a unit square and the latest square of side 2—having sides 3 units long; and then another touching both the square of size and the square of size 3 (which has sides of 5 units).

We can continue adding squares around the picture, each new square having a side as long as the sum of the latest two squares' sides. This set of rectangles, whose sides are two successive Fibonacci numbers in length and which are composed of squares with sides that are Fibonacci numbers, we will call *Fibonacci rectangles* (see Figure 10-2).

Figure 10-3 shows that we can draw a spiral by putting together quarter circles, one in each new square. This is a spiral (the *Fibonacci spiral*). A curve that is similar to this occurs in nature as the shape of a snail shell or the nautilus seashell.

Whereas a Fibonacci spiral increases in size by a factor of phi (Phi is approximately 1.618), in a *quarter turn* (i.e., a point a further quarter turn around the curve is 1.618 times as far from the center, and this applies to *all* points on the curve) the nautilus spiral curve takes a *whole turn* before points move a factor of 1.618 from the center. These spiral shapes are called *equiangular* or *logarithmic spirals*.

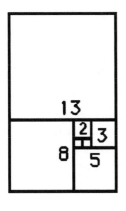

FIGURE 10-2   Fibonacci Rectangles

FIGURE 10-3   Fibonacci Shell Spirals

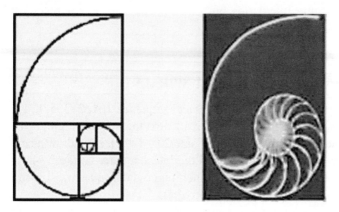

FIBONACCI RETRACEMENTS

A Fibonacci retracement is tool used to measure the amount the market has retraced compared with overall market movement. Fibonacci retracements give you support and resistance areas along with general target prices.

As shown in Figure 10-4, the lines start at the beginning of a wave and are dragged to the top of the same wave as prices retrace. A target entry point occurs when prices touch the 0.618 line and begin to return toward the long-term trend.

Fibonacci retracements commonly are drawn from the beginning of wave 1, the zero point, to the top or bottom of wave 2 to find a target for the beginning of wave 3. The default retracement percentages are 25, 38.2, 50, and 61.8 (see Figure 10-5).

FIBONACCI EXTENSIONS

Fibonacci extensions are used to measure the amount a market may extend compared with overall movement. Fibonacci extensions give you general target price areas.

Fibonacci extensions are used most often to find the general area of wave 5. You would click on the start of a wave 1 (the zero point), then click on the top of wave 2, and then click one more time at the beginning of wave 3. The default percentage extensions are 61.8, 100, 161.8, and 261.8 (see Figures 10-6 and 10-7).

FIGURE 10-4   Fibonacci Retracements

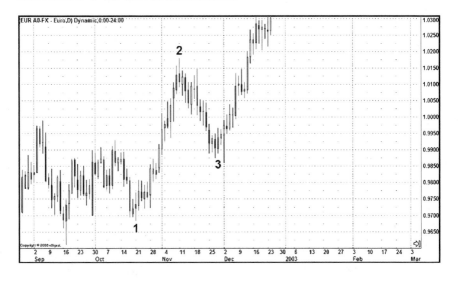

FIGURE 10-5   Fibonacci Retracements

FIBONACCI TIME

Fibonacci time is a tool used between two price points to estimate a future price at a particular time. Clicking your mouse from one high to another will give you an idea of when the third high should be expected. Figures 10-8 and 10-9 provide an example.

FIGURE 10-6 Fibonacci Retracements

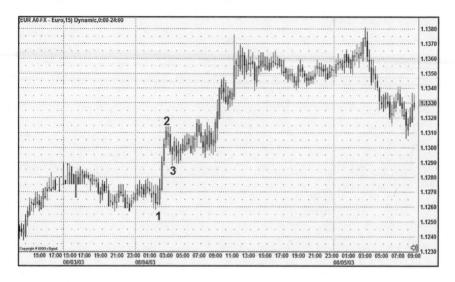

FIGURE 10-7 Fibonacci Extension

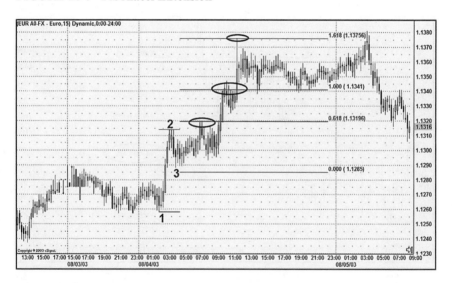

FIBONACCI CIRCLES

A Fibonacci circle is a combination of a Fibonacci retracement/extension and Fibonacci time. By drawing a circle from the top to the bottom of the last trend, we can identify potential support and resistance levels and time frames in which to expect them.

FIGURE 10-8   Fibonacci Time

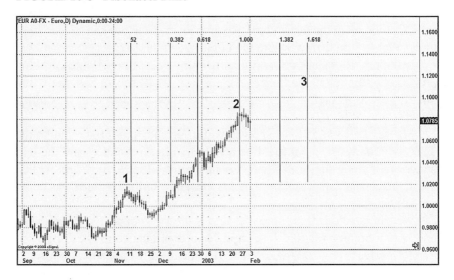

FIGURE 10-9   Fibonacci Time

By clicking and dragging your mouse from the most recent highs or lows to the beginning of that trend, the Fibonacci circle can help you to identify the immediate support, resistance, or trend reversals. In Figures 10-10 through 10-12, the top of the trend is identified by Figure 10-10 and the bottom by Figure 10-11.

We can see in Figure 10-10 that the long-term trend is bullish. We also can see that the top is starting to flatten out and that a possible trend reversal is coming up in the near future. By drawing a circle, we can set out stop-limit orders a little below where the circle shows support.

In Figure 10-11 an arrow points to our target support, and our stop limit is slightly below that price level. Figure 10-12 shows how the 0.382 line did act as strong support and that the trend continued in its bullish direction.

Figures 10-13 and 10-14 show how the currency pair broke though the 0.382 line; however, the 0.618 line acted as strong resistance, and the pair traded right along the rim of that resistance until it broke through. At that point, the currency pair started a new trend, and a bullish pattern was being developed.

We can conclude that the 0.382 line is the first support and resistance line, and a bounce off that line signifies a continuance of the long-term trend. However, the breaking of the 0.618 line usually indicates a new trend in the making.

FIGURE 10-10   Fibonacci Circle

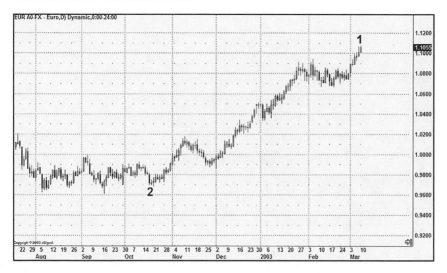

FIGURE 10-11   Fibonacci Circle

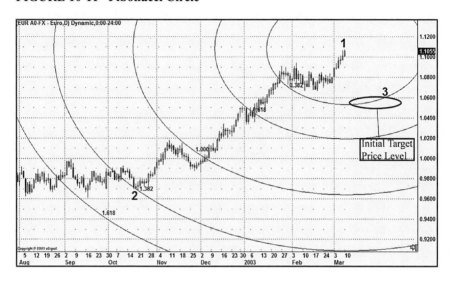

FIGURE 10-12   Fibonacci Circle

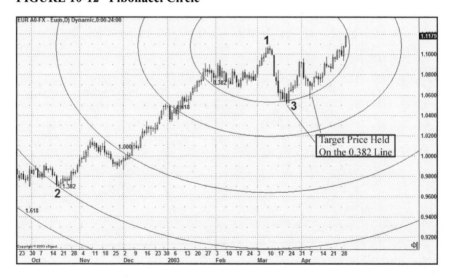

FIGURE 10-13 Fibonacci Circle

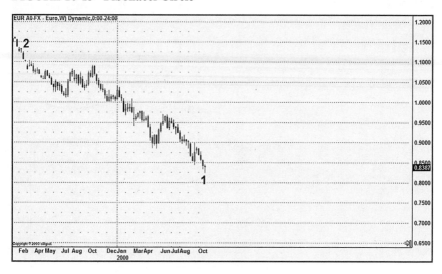

FIGURE 10-14 Fibonacci Circle

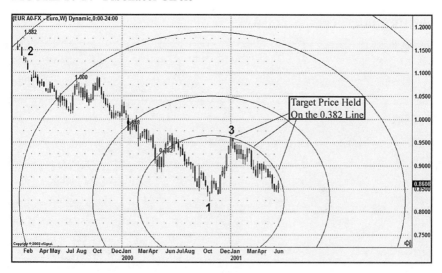

ELLIOT WAVES

> Practically all developments which result from (human) social-economic processes follow a law that causes them to repeat themselves in similar and constantly recurring serials of waves or impulses of definite number and pattern.
>
> *R. N. Elliott, in Nature's Law: The Secret of the*
> *Universe*

R. N. Elliott discerned various types of wave patterns and labeled them. He discovered that there were two basic types of wave patterns: (1) waves that move in the direction of the main trend of the market, that is, *impulse waves* consisting of five smaller waves, and (2) waves that move counter to the market's main direction, that is, *corrective waves* consisting of three smaller waves.

He further discovered that each wave, whether impulsive or corrective, subdivides into smaller waves and/or is part of a larger wave. Waves therefore can be analyzed in time periods ranging from a matter of minutes to months and years.

The most difficult part of Elliott wave analysis is correctly labeling and counting the waves. A correct wave count can lead the analyst to amazing accuracy in forecasting the market. An incorrect wave count, of course, will have the opposite result.

Wave counting is quite subjective and usually will result in as many forecasts as there are Elliott wave forecasters. Because of this, it is often said by its harshest critics that Elliott wave analysis is useful only in hindsight, which is to say that it is not very useful in predicting the future course of the market.

I respectfully disagree. I have found that simplicity, proportionality, and flexibility in wave counting lead to the best results. Your ability is constantly challenged by the market and is always evolving, hopefully to a higher level.

Even if you are not interested in Elliott wave analysis as a trading technique for short-term profits, an understanding of Elliott waves still has value because it brings to the investor a sense of historical perspective.

Markets never go in one direction forever. Markets that go up eventually do come down. Unlike any other form of analysis that I know of, the sheer power of Elliott wave analysis as a forecasting tool creates a great deal of confusion and worry about the market.

It goes without saying that the followers of this form of analysis believe that market timing is critical. It is up to you to decide whether market timing should be a consideration when you make your own investment decisions.

IMPULSE WAVES

An impulse wave is a wave that moves in the direction of the main trend of the market. It subdivides into five smaller waves. Waves 1, 3, and 5 move in the direction of the market's main trend. Waves 2 and 4 move against the market's main trend. (They are called *corrective waves.*)

Basic Five-Wave Structure

> *Wave 1.* The currency pair makes its initial move upward. This is usually caused by a relatively small number of people who all of a sudden feel that the previous price of the pair was cheap and therefore the pair is worth buying, causing the price to go up.

> *Wave 2.* The currency pair is considered overvalued. At this point, enough people who were in the original wave consider the pair overvalued and start taking profits. This causes the price of the pair to go down.

> *Wave 3.* This is usually the longest and strongest wave. More people have found out about the currency pair. More people want the pair, and they buy it for a higher and higher price. This wave usually exceeds the tops created at the end of wave 1.

> *Wave 4.* At this point, people again take profits because the currency pair is again considered expensive.

> *Wave 5.* This is the point where most people get on the currency pair, and the price is most driven by hysteria. People will come up with lots of reasons to buy the pair and won't listen to reasons not to. This is the point where the pair becomes the most overpriced. At this point it will move into one of two patterns, either it will move toward a correction (a-b-c) (see Figure 10-16) or it will start over again with wave 1 (see Figure 10-15).

Here are some additional terms that apply to impulse waves:

Extended wave. A complex impulse wave in which one of the subwaves (either 1, 3, or 5) further subdivides into five waves.

Failure. This occurs when the fifth subwave of an impulse wave fails to move beyond the end of the third subwave, indicating a strong and/or prolonged move in the opposite direction.

Diagonal triangle. This is a terminal wave (often called a *wedge*), either a fifth wave or a c wave, in which the five subwaves subdivide into threes (a-b-c). On completion, there is usually a strong move in the opposite direction.

FIGURE 10-15   Elliott Impulse Wave

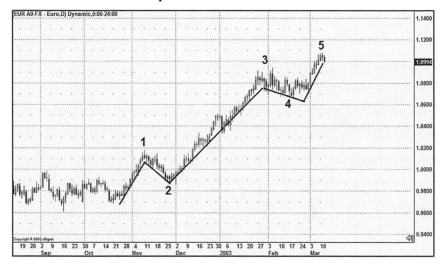

FIGURE 10-16   Elliott Corrective Wave

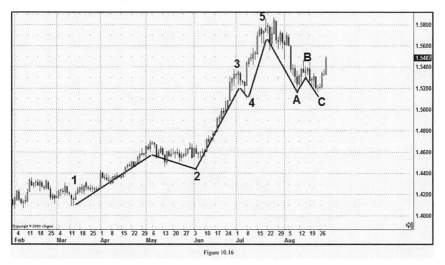

Figure 10.16

CORRECTIVE WAVES

A corrective wave is a wave that moves counter to the direction of the main trend of the market. It subdivides into three smaller waves (a-b-c). Waves a and c move against the market's main trend. Wave b moves in the direction of the market's main trend but subdivides into three waves (see Figure 10-16).

Here are some additional terms that apply to corrective waves:

Zigzag. A corrective wave (a-b-c) in which the b wave retraces only a part of wave a, and wave c moves beyond the terminal point of wave a. Waves a and c subdivide into five waves and wave b into three waves. (*Double zigzags* are two zigzags in succession connected by an *x* wave.)

Flat. A corrective wave (a-b-c) in which the b wave retraces all or more of wave a. Wave a subdivides into three waves, and wave c may or may not terminate beyond the terminal point of wave a.

Horizontal triangle. A corrective wave (a-b-c-d-e) that often develops after a very strong move in the market with five subwaves, each further subdividing into threes, that is, five successive corrective patterns forming a sideways pattern in the market (more or less).

Combination. A prolonged corrective wave that combines into one larger corrective wave—two or three corrective waves that are connected by one or two *x* waves. Two corrective waves connected by an *x* wave are called a *double three.* Three corrective patterns each connected by an *x* wave are called a *triple three.* The *x* wave, like other corrective waves in the direction of the main trend, subdivides into three waves (a-b-c).

OTHER ELLIOTT WAVE CONCEPTS

Wave degree. Each five-wave and three-wave cycle can be found to subdivide into waves of a smaller scale and/or be found to consist of a part of a wave of a larger scale. Waves can be labeled in degrees that last only a matter of minutes or as long as centuries.

Parallel trendlines. Waves tend to channel between parallel trendlines. Depending on the time period analyzed, the market may channel between parallel trendlines on an arithmetic-scale chart or on a semilog-scale chart.

Extent of corrective wave. Generally, a corrective wave will take the market to the area of wave 4 of one lesser degree, especially when the corrective wave itself is a fourth wave. In other cases, the market often will find support at the top of wave 1 of one lesser degree.

Rule of equality. Two of the subwaves of an impulse wave (waves 1, 3, or 5) are often related equally in terms of price advance and time.

Rule of alternation. Waves, especially corrective waves, tend to vary in complexity and/or type from one to the next.

11

MONEY MANAGEMENT PRINCIPLES

- Trade with Sufficient Capital
- Exercise Discipline
- Be Patient and Persistent
- Employ Risk-to-Reward Ratios
- Follow Trading Rules
- Accept Losses
- Always, Always Use Stops
- When in Doubt, Stay Out
- Never Overleverage Your Account
- Make Realistic Goals That Can Be Achieved within Reason
- Always Trade with Money You Can Afford to Lose
- Protect Your Profits
- Keep a Trading Log

TRADE WITH SUFFICIENT CAPITAL

One of the worst blunders that traders can make is attempting to trade without sufficient capital. This does not mean that you have to have a lot of money, but you have to have enough to handle the movement in the market or you increase your chance of getting blown out.

The trader with limited capital not only will be a worried trader, always looking to minimize losses beyond the point of realistic trading, but he or she also frequently will be taken out of the trading game before he or she can realize any sense of success trading the system.

The minimum required amount to open a foreign exchange market (FOREX) trading account is $2000, but I recommend that you start with $5000 to $10,000 in a regular account. A miniaccount can be opened with as little as $300 if more capital is not available; however, I recommend that you open a miniaccount with at least $5000.

A *regular account*—most often referred to as a *100k account*—allows you to trade with lot sizes equal to $100,000. Each lot is worth $100,000 in currency. It will take $1000 to trade one lot. This is a 1 percent margin.

You can change the margin amount to whatever you feel most comfortable with from a risk perspective. When you open your account, you should determine what the default margin is or you may get one with a greater or lesser degree of risk than you are willing to accept.

If you start at a 2 percent margin, then it will cost you $2000 to place a one-lot trade. As discussed in earlier chapters, currency moves in price interest points (pips), and in a regular (100k) account, each pip is worth about $8 to $10. This is different in a miniaccount.

The *miniaccount* was developed to accommodate investors looking for an alternative to the stock market for diversification purposes. The small-dollar requirement of the miniaccount allows many investors to participate in FOREX who previously were unable to do so.

A miniaccount uses a different leverage calculation than a regular account. Instead of a lot controlling $100,000, the miniaccount lot is $10,000. Instead of $1000 or a 1 percent margin in a regular (100k) account, you need only $50.

Pips in a miniaccount are worth, on average, $1 instead of the $10 in a regular (100k) account. This provides investors of all types with an easy way to get started trading in the FOREX.

EXERCISE DISCIPLINE

Discipline is probably one of the most overused words in trading education. However, despite the cliché, discipline continues to be the most important behavior one can master to become a profitable trader.

Discipline is the ability to plan your work and work your plan. It is the ability to give your trade the time to develop without hastily taking yourself out of the market simply because you are uncomfortable with risk. Discipline is also the ability to continue to trade your system even after you have suffered a loss. Do your best to cultivate the degree of discipline required to be a world-class trader.

BE PATIENT AND PERSISTENT

Many traders have become sorely disappointed when they have not attained immediate success. Be consistent in allowing yourself sufficient time to achieve success. Persistence is one of the most important qualities a trader can possess.

Short-term trading requires the ability to continue on even when your trading results are not good. Some of a trader's greatest successes occur right after a string of losses. Those who quit too soon or apply their system haphazardly will not be trading in the market enough to allow their system to produce the wins they are looking for.

To develop persistence, you must force yourself initially to do everything according to the rules of your trading method or system. Follow through on this commitment, and you will find that after you have taken every trade according to your tested system, your consistency will have paid off, and you will have profits to show for your efforts.

EMPLOY RISK-TO-REWARD RATIOS

Most beginning traders believe that a good entry into the market is the key to success. Unfortunately, most are very wrong. Money management is by far the most important criterion of trading, no matter what you are trading. Every successful trader will agree that managing your trades correctly is the number 1 key to consistent profits.

A *risk-to-reward ratio* compares the potential for reward against the potential for loss. A trader must view his or her trade as a business transaction. *Risk* is identified by counting the pips between the forecasted entry price and the forecasted price at which one would exit the market in a losing trade. *Reward* is identified by counting the pips between the forecasted entry price and the forecasted price at which one would exit the market in a winning trade. To manage risk effectively, it is necessary to find high-probability trades that have a 1:1.5 or greater risk-to-reward ratio. This depends largely on the time frame you are looking to trade.

The longer time chart, such as a day, week, or month, requires you to be willing to accept a larger drawdown. For example, if you are using an active setting and your profit potential is only 30 pips, you may want to set your stop loss at about 15 pips from entry. However, with a longer time frame, your profit potential will be 200 pips, and you will need to set your stops at around 100 pips.

The reason you need to set larger stop limits with a longer time frame is that small trends occur with large trends. A retracement on a short time interval is much smaller compared with a long-term interval. Your trade is going to recycle, and in order for you not to be stopped out, you have to absorb the loss of the recycling. Therefore, you need to calculate the risk-to-reward ratio appropriately.

Traders agree that the most important thing, next to maximizing profits, is minimizing losses. Yet precious little is actually written about this vital aspect of trading. A trading system or method that wins only 50 percent of the time can still be extremely profitable.

Now I can hear most of you saying to yourselves, "How can you make the huge returns if you are only profitable 50 percent of the time?" It is really very simple—*money management.* You see, if you are able to manage your money effectively, you only need to be right about 50 percent of the time.

The unfortunate thing about 90 percent of today's traders is that their primary focus tends to be on making money and not on protecting what they currently have. You have a 50/50 chance of the market going your way just by flipping a coin. In the event that a trade does not develop in a reasonable amount of time or the market begins to form an opposite setup, you should employ the strategy of *cutting your losses short* to protect and preserve your capital. In short, you cut your losses short and let your winners run. This simple strategy lets 50/50 trading earn a profit when a novice trader might experience a loss.

The following table shows possible risk-to-reward ratios and the win ratios required to break even in a trading system.

Risk-to-Reward Ratio (in pips)	Win Ratio Required to Break Even
40/20 (2:1)	67%
40/40 (1:1)	50%
40/60 (1:1.5)	40%
40/80 (1:2)	33.5%
60/20 (3:1)	75%
60/60 (1:1)	50%
60/90 (1:1.5)	40%
60/120 (1:2)	33.5%

In order to use risk-to-reward ratios effectively, you must study the method you plan to employ and then *backtest* the system and determine how accurate it is. When backtesting, consider that market conditions change from period to period and therefore that you must take strong trends and nontrends into account. Then you must evaluate how much you can risk per trade based on your trading account.

Typically, you should not enter a position with more than 10 to 15 percent of your cash position and a stop loss of no more than 3 to 5 percent of your account. Find the right balance for yourself in the beginning, and you will be a step ahead of the game.

In the trade log shown in Figure 11-1, note that the trader has made 10 trades. Half the trades are successful, and half the trades are not. In the end, however, because the trader has cut his or her losses short, the account winds up with a $1000 trading profit, all because of good money management.

FOLLOW TRADING RULES

The proper execution of trades is one of the most important aspects of becoming a profitable trader and one of the most difficult to learn. The problem comes with the initial analysis of a market. When you are studying examples of past trades, it is much easier to recognize direction, entries, and exits than if you are trading live.

Recognizing opportunity in the "now" is much more difficult to do. To develop this skill, you must pay very close attention to specific price patterns and the chart positions of indicators.

FIGURE 11-1   Sample trade log (hypothetical, of course)

Buy USD/JPY ($200)
Sell GBP/USD ($200)
Buy USD/CHF (+$400)
Sell EUR/USD ($200)
Sell USD/JPY (+$400)
Buy EUR/USD (+$400)
Buy USD/CHF (+$400)
Sell GBP/USD ($200)
Buy USD/JPY ($200)
Sell EUR/USD (+$400)
Net profits: $1000

Following trading rules and a trading system is no easy task. It requires discipline for a trader to obey the rule that he or she is following even when the initial response or the opening trade does not work out. Trading rules are not perfect, and they will all fail you at times.

The successful trader learns to overcome the emotion and continue to follow the rule that he or she believes in, knowing the odds are now in his or her favor. Trading should occur only when the right setups are present and when confidence is high.

ACCEPT LOSSES

Losses are going to happen in the course of trading. Since no trading system is 100 percent accurate, even the flawless application of a trading system will create some losses. Develop the ability to admit to your losses.

Sometimes traders will remove their stops and let their losses run. They do this because they are unwilling to admit that their forecast of market direction or their timing of entry into the market was incorrect.

Losses occur primarily for two reasons. The first is when the trader fails to follow established tested rules and guidelines of a trading system. The second is when the trading system fails to encompass unexpected changes in market conditions. In either case, by anticipating the reasons for most of the losses you are going to take, you can put precautions into place beforehand to help reduce losses in the future.

ALWAYS, ALWAYS USE STOPS

Stops are orders in the market placed a distance from your entry price in the event that market prices turn and move dramatically opposite from the anticipated direction. The idea behind a stop is to prevent a loss from "running" too far and thereby consuming excessive capital in one single trade.

Too often traders are so convinced of where they believe market prices are headed that they lose their sense of reality and begin to trade on hope. They choose not to trade with a stop or remove their stop, *hoping* that market direction eventually will turn *their* way and their loss will turn into a win.

By the time the realization comes that the market or position is not going to move upward and that their hope was an illusion, they have risked far more than they wanted to at the outset of their trade, and the result is a devastating, excessive loss. Be wise and follow the experts: *Always use stops.*

Most traders in the past, even the greatest ones, have always suffered the most in a time of quick uncertainty, such as the September 11 terrorist attacks in New York and Washington. Catastrophic events will have a tremendous effect on the market. Using a stop will allow you to be taken out of the market and sit on the side until things even out a bit. You can always get back in, but once all your money is gone, it is gone!

These strategies are not just for the FOREX. They are good for all markets that you trade. If stock traders were to follow the same strategy of using stops, most of the traders to whom I have spoken over the last few years would have been far better off and had more capital to enter the market again.

WHEN IN DOUBT, STAY OUT

If you come to a point in your market analysis in any trading session where you have no confidence as to an accurate forecast of market direction, simply choose not to trade. The old saying "A lost opportunity is better than lost capital" is true.

In such cases, wait for market conditions to become clearer, and increase the probability of success by trading when trade setups are strong. This is far more important to understand in the FOREX than in the stock market.

The FOREX moves a lot more, and the leverage allows you to have the opportunity to make a lot more money much faster. Therefore, if you do not see the opportunity to get in, you can afford to sit on the sidelines. Learn to be a patient trader and let the market come to you.

NEVER OVERLEVERAGE YOUR ACCOUNT

Leverage is another key to making money in the FOREX. No other market in the world allows the leverage that this incredible market offers. Normally, 100:1 leverage is the amount that most brokerages allow investors to trade with. For each $1000 that you put up in cash, the brokerage allows you to control $100,000 worth of currency.

Think about this for a moment. It is really incredible. The broker has loaned you $99,000 dollars secured only by your $1000. This huge leverage is what allows you the potential to make the kinds of returns that the FOREX offers. However, it also enables you to lose some or all of your money if you trade foolishly.

Leverage is a wonderful moneymaking tool, but when it is abused, it can lead to financial destruction as well. Think about consumer credit cards, for example. The bank lets you borrow large sums of money on your word that you will pay it back, but when credit is abused, it can lead to bankruptcy for many. Therefore, just like managing your credit-card debt, you need to manage your trading leverage.

Most people would not go out and rack up huge debt that they knew they could not pay because it would not be responsible, right? Well, when trading the FOREX, if you started with a $10,000 account, should you start by trading 10 lots using all your cash? No, that also would be foolish.

A very conservative yet very effective method of trading is to never leverage more than 20 percent of your account at any one time. Thus, with $10,000, you realistically should only trade two lots. Using good money management and discipline, you could quickly grow your account in a relatively short amount of time.

The compounding factor of money is a very powerful thing. Because many people have a desire to get rich quick, they take unnecessary risks and tend to focus more on the dollar signs than on proper trading principles.

If you truly want to make consistent profits and exceptional returns on your hard-earned money, take it from someone who has been there: Follow these simple but effective money management rules.

If you are starting with a miniaccount, start by trading only one position of a tenth of a lot. You will not able to make huge money, because the position size is only one-tenth of a normal account, but the percentage of returns will quickly allow you to start trading larger sums of money and, in the end, will allow you the success you seek.

MAKE REALISTIC GOALS THAT CAN BE ACHIEVED WITHIN REASON

Emotions and money do not mix. Simply treat each trade as a business transaction and don't get emotionally attached to a trade. When you have a loss, take it and move on. Don't beat yourself up over it.

Learning how to lose is probably more important than winning, because a new trader typically will take the first loss, wonder what he or she did wrong, and then sit on the sidelines and let all the profitable trades go by. Discipline is a key factor in trading, and it is a learned trait. It takes a bit of time to get used to, so accept your losses and move on. Once you have proven it to yourself, trust the software or trade system you are using to take you through the winning trades.

ALWAYS TRADE WITH MONEY YOU CAN AFFORD TO LOSE

Trading with money you cannot afford to lose is a very foolish thing to do, yet it is common among beginning traders. When trading, be sure to trade only with money that will not affect your lifestyle. You are trying to improve your lifestyle, not hamper it.

When a trader trades with money that he or she can afford to lose, he or she tends to be more focused and more disciplined. Such a trader is not worried about any single loss. Simply, he or she is looking forward to the overall return.

Don't borrow money to trade on. Don't use your life savings. And don't use the money that you would use to pay your monthly bills. This is just a road to disaster. Traders who do this have the same mentality that gamblers have. Remember this: Traders are *not* gamblers. If you must compare trading to gambling, then compare yourself to the casino owners. As a disciplined trader, you trade with probabilities on your side so that in the end, like the casino owners, you will come out way ahead.

PROTECT YOUR PROFITS

Protecting your profits is another factor that helps to ensure consistent success. If you are a longer-term trader such as a swing trader or position trader, it is important to protect your profits by using a trailing stop loss. For example, let's say that you are taking a long position (buying) in the USD/JPY and you are looking for a larger return than $400. Now let's say that your goal is $800 rather than $400, and you are currently sitting at a $500 profit.

Most professional traders would take this opportunity to trail their stop loss to at least an even position or, better yet, to lock in a portion of these profits so that they have no chance of taking a loss. Remember, however, that your goal is $800 or a loss of, let's say, $400, a 2:1 risk-to-reward ratio.

Let's assume that the market, for whatever reason, starts making a large move against your position. If you protected at least a portion of the trade or moved your stop to breakeven position, then you would have avoided at least one loss that you were not willing to risk in the first place.

KEEP A TRADING LOG

Keeping a log of trades is like taking a snapshot in time. You will find that after making your first analysis, market conditions develop so rapidly that it can be difficult to remember exactly what you saw in the beginning that caused you to enter the market. By recording just a few notes about each trade you make and the technical picture you see, you will sharpen your skills in recognizing strong trade setups.

As a convenience, most trading software keeps track of all the detailed information of your trades, including times, open prices, closing prices, and so on. A detailed trading log, along with good trading software reports, offers the trader a complete picture of trades for later analysis.

Trading the FOREX, as you can see, has a tremendous amount of possibilities. You have to use good common sense when you trade. This market moves so much that you will not sit in a trade and watch it do nothing.

You often will see currency pairs trade in ranges, whether big ones or short ones. Practice good money management and use good risk management, and you will see the opportunities transpire.

12

SIX STEPS TO SUCCESS

- Identify Current Long- and Short-Term Trends and Which Trend to Trade

- Check News and Market Announcements

- Identify Support and Resistance Levels

- Use Studies and Indicators for Entry

- Buy at Dip Bottoms (Uptrends) or Sell on Rally Tops (Downtrend)

- Use Proper Money Management

IDENTIFY CURRENT LONG- AND SHORT-TERM TRENDS AND WHICH TREND TO TRADE

As a foreign exchange market (FOREX) trader, you will quickly get comfortable with the time intervals you find most appealing to your style of trading. While there is no specific time frame that works 100 percent of the time, I strongly recommend that you start with a long-term chart and work your way down to a short-term chart.

By analyzing a daily chart first, you will be able to determine the long-term trend. This long-term trend will be one of three trends—an upward,

149

downward, or sideways trend. Determining a possible position trade on a daily chart will help you to look for specific indicators in shorter-time-interval charts for entry time and price.

If a daily chart does not show an upward or downward direction, you can work your way down to a 180- or 60-minute chart and look for a possible swing trade. This follows the same pattern all the way down to superactive traders, who use minute charts for entry and exit signals.

Picking a trend is one of the first and most important decisions you will make after reviewing the long- and short-term trends and checking what announcements and market news are coming up in the near future. The maxim "The trend is your friend" holds true today as it has in the past and is the number 1 tool used in history.

It is crucial to follow a trend and not anticipate one with an early entry. While studying charts and intervals, you may notice a possible trend reversal. Don't trade until that trend develops.

CHECK NEWS AND MARKET ANNOUNCEMENTS

The FOREX is driven largely by the world financial markets and domestic and international news. It is very important to stay on top of breaking news, economic announcements, and monthly and weekly reports. As an example, every month the U.S. markets report unemployment rate, consumer confidence, and gross domestic product (GDP), which have huge impacts on the U.S. dollar.

A good trading strategy to follow is make sure that you are comfortable with the potential news if you plan to enter a trade before the news comes out. If you do decide to enter a trade prior to news being announced, make sure that you have your stops placed.

Some news will affect the market very quickly and very drastically. Other events, such as wars, government elections, holidays, and even bad weather, may have significant impacts that may be unique to each currency pair in the FOREX.

Getting to know the behavior of currency pairs is very important. The U.S. dollar, for instance, is directly related to the price of gold or oil. The Japanese yen is sometimes controlled partially by the Bank of Japan (BOJ) to stay within a certain range to promote Japan's large export industry.

Such examples can be found on almost all the major currencies, and owing to the differences in behavior of currency pairs, I recommend that you get to know several of them in depth and trade only those. Knowing how and why certain currency pairs act the way they do will give you insight and possibly increase your profits.

IDENTIFY SUPPORT AND RESISTANCE LEVELS

Support and resistance levels are very important to identify and use correctly. These levels are used not only to determine entry and exit prices but also in setting stop-loss and limit orders.

Many trend reversals occur directly after a bounce off a major support or resistance price level. Properly identifying these price levels will help you to understand why a currency is changing trends. Many beginning traders ask why the currency changes trend just as they enter into it. Well, these support and resistance levels are a huge factor for these trend reversals.

USE STUDIES AND INDICATORS FOR ENTRY

A proper entry into a position is one of the most important parts of trading any market. By being able to use several charts and indicators, you will make better decisions for profitable trades. It is important to have indicators that show the same trends and to avoid entering a position where indicators show mixed signals. Look for a strong confirmation by a couple of indicators before you enter a position.

As you look at long- or short-term trends, check the indicators such as the moving average convergence and divergence (MAC/D), the relative strength indicator (RSI), and the stochastic indicator for possible overbought or oversold signals. Even though the currency pair is strong one way or another and there may not be a support or resistance price level in the near future, the pair may be in an overbought or oversold condition, making a reversal a distinct possibility.

BUY AT DIP BOTTOMS (UPTRENDS) OR SELL ON RALLY TOPS (DOWNTRENDS)

While the market moves in trends, it has its small retracement trends. To maximize your potential profits, you should enter or add to your positions at dip bottoms or rally tops (see Figures 12-1 and 12-2). This will allow you to enter stop limits for a true trend reversal and avoid getting stopped out by a retracement. Resistance and support levels will help you with determining the retracements and possible entry points.

The use of Fibonacci retracement tools will help you in calculating a buy or sell price and in determining the currency pair's retracement potential. I strongly advise you to look at the currency pair's trend history to determine what the retracement percentage usually is.

USE PROPER MONEY MANAGEMENT

The use of money management is the last step on your road to success—but perhaps the most important. Proper money management minimizes capital loss and maximizes profits. I cannot stress enough that the proper use of money management will be the ultimate tool and key in your success in the FOREX.

As I mentioned earlier, trading with sufficient capital is very important. This will allow you to stay in positions as they develop and not force you to take quick profits and losses. Be patient. Employ risk-to-reward ratios that will allow you to be profitable in the long run, even if you have several positions that did not have a profitable outcome.

Follow the same rules each and every time, and accept your losses. Trading in the FOREX or any other market with money you cannot afford to lose is never a wise idea. It will make you a nervous trader, and emotions will start running your trades. Last but not least, always use stop limits!

FIGURE 12-1 EUR/USD Daily Chart 2002–2003

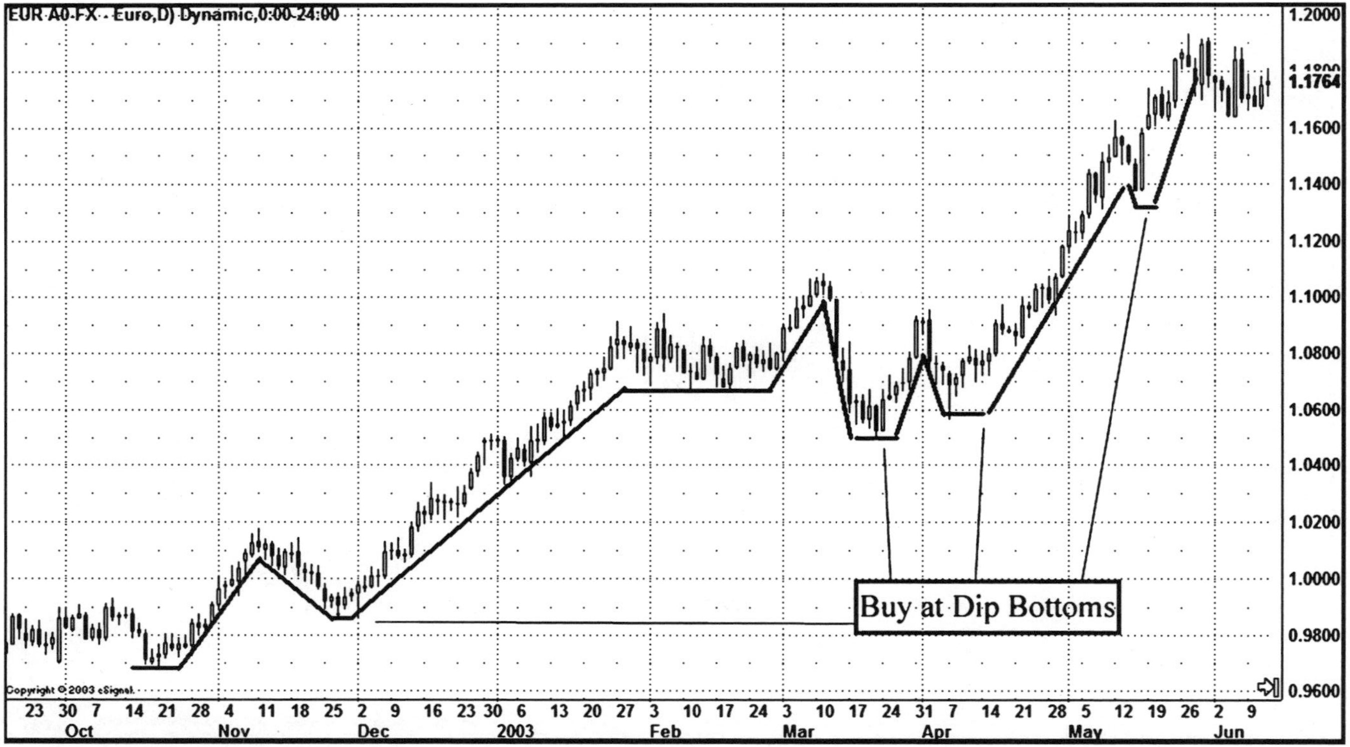

153

FIGURE 12-2 USD/CHF 180-Minute Chart 2002–2003

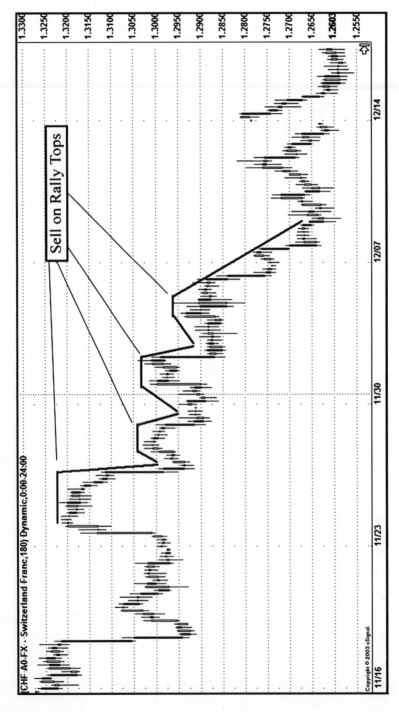

13

GETTING STARTED WITH A TRADING STATION

- Access the PremiereTrade Web Site
- Install and Run the Dealing Software
- Open a Demo Trading Account
- Dealing Rates Window
- Open Positions Window
- Accounts Window
- Multiple-Accounts Window
- Order Window
- Placing a Market Order
- Placing a Stop/Limit on Open Position
- Change Price on a Stop/Limit (Open Position)

- Delete a Stop/Limit on Open Position
- Close an Open Position
- Placing an Entry Order
- Change an Entry Order
- Canceling an Entry Order
- Reports
- Customizing the Trading Screen
- Trading Station Options

ACCESS THE PREMIERETRADE WEB SITE

The PremiereTrade Web site is a very helpful resource. There you will find special announcements, daily analyses, file or program downloads, online lessons and tutorials, scheduled classes, and other useful information. To access this area, go to the PremiereTrade Web site at *www.premieretrade.com.*

INSTALL AND RUN THE DEALING SOFTWARE

Follow the online instructions and links to download the PremiereTrade Dealing Station. By installing this software, you will be able to place trades, review foreign exchange market (FOREX) news, analyze charts, and study indicators.

You will need either a real or demo account. When you download the PremiereTrade Dealing Station with its step-by-step instructions, you also will be instructed on obtaining a user name and password.

Should you have any questions or difficulties with downloading or installing the PremiereTrade Dealing Station program, you can contact the technical support staff through the PremiereTrade Web site.

OPEN A DEMO TRADING ACCOUNT

You can obtain a demo trading account online at the PremiereTrade Web site. After you register, you will receive a user name and password by e-mail. Go to *www.premieretrade.com,* and then follow the tutorials.

After you have accessed your new demo account, follow the tutorials for step-by-step instructions on how to begin placing practice orders.

Within 30 days of the first time you successfully access your charts, you will need to open your live trading account. Follow the instructions at the end of the broker tutorial to open your real, live trading account.

If you have problems receiving a demo trading account user name and password, installing your demo account, or accessing your demo account for the first time, after reading the tutorials, contact PremiereTrade directly. A list of contact numbers is available on the Web site.

DEALING RATES WINDOW

Figure 13-1 shows the Dealing Rates window.

CURRENCY

Each row in the Dealing Rates window contains information about a specific currency pair. In the first column, the currency pair is defined. There is a three-letter abbreviation for each currency. For example, *EUR/USD* stands for the euro/U.S. dollar currency pair. The first currency listed in every pair is the *base currency*.

FIGURE 13-1   Dealing Rates

Currency	Sell	Buy	High	Low	IntrS	IntrB	Time
EUR/USD	0.9890	0.9894	0.9910	0.9832	-4.00	2.00	13:13
USD/JPY	122.62	122.67	123.25	122.31	-5.00	2.50	13:11
GBP/USD	1.5636	1.5641	1.5658	1.5557	-9.00	4.00	13:13
USD/CHF	1.4782	1.4787	1.4895	1.4753	-3.00	1.50	13:13
EUR/CHF	1.4621	1.4628	1.4657	1.4609	-7.00	3.00	13:13
AUD/USD	0.5543	0.5548	0.5556	0.5521	-4.50	2.50	13:07
USD/CAD	1.5609	1.5614	1.5710	1.5582	1.00	-2.50	13:08
NZD/USD	0.4853	0.4860	0.4868	0.4820	-5.00	2.50	13:06
EUR/GBP	0.6323	0.6328	0.6341	0.6311	0.75	-1.50	13:13
EUR/JPY	121.30	121.35	121.46	120.73	-9.00	4.50	13:13
GBP/JPY	191.75	191.85	192.01	190.75	-17.00	8.00	13:13
CHF/JPY	82.91	83.01	83.09	82.44	-2.00	1.00	13:12
GBP/CHF	2.3113	2.3128	2.3206	2.3080	-14.00	7.00	13:13
EUR/AUD	1.7828	1.7848	1.7877	1.7770	2.00	-3.50	13:13
EUR/CAD	1.5438	1.5448	1.5528	1.5393	-2.00	1.00	13:13
AUD/CAD	0.8652	0.8662	0.8704	0.8642	-3.00	1.50	13:07
AUD/JPY	67.96	68.06	68.19	67.61	-7.50	3.75	13:11

The *exchange rate* refers to the amount of the second currency that can be exchanged for one unit of the base currency. For example, if the exchange rate for the EUR/USD is 0.9800, then US$0.9800 (98 cents) can be exchanged for 1 euro.

SELL AND BUY
Each row contains two five-digit numbers following identification of the currency pair. The first number appears under the column entitled "Sell." This is the market exchange rate that can be executed immediately to sell. The trader is selling the base currency and buying the second currency.

When executing a sell order, the trader expects the exchange rate to go down. For example, a trader executing a sell of EUR/USD at 0.9500 would like the exchange rate to move toward zero.

The next column to the right of the "Sell" column is the "Buy" column. This is the market price that can be executed immediately to buy the base currency and sell the second currency. When executing a buy order, the trader expects the exchange rate to move higher.

The "Sell" and "Buy" exchange rates move in tandem. When the exchange rates are moving higher, the numbers are red. When they are moving lower, the exchange rates turn blue.

HIGH AND LOW
The next columns following "Buy" and "Sell" are entitled "High," meaning high offer (buy), and "Low," meaning ask (sell). The high is the highest the bid rate has reached since 5:00 P.M. EST the previous day. The low is the lowest the offer rate has reached since 5:00 P.M. EST the previous day.

INTEREST RATE B AND INTEREST RATE S
At 5:00 P.M. EST, traders with open positions have their positions automatically rolled over to the next settlement date. If a trader has no open positions at 5:00 P.M. EST, even if the trader executed transactions during the previous 24 hours, there will be no rollover of positions.

A rollover of positions will result in funds being added to or subtracted from the trader's account. The amount changes day to day for each currency pair depending on market conditions. At 3:00 P.M. EST, the rollover amounts are posted for each currency pair.

Under the "IntrB" column, the amount in U.S. dollars per $100,000 buy position is provided. If there is a minus sign next to the number, the amount will be subtracted. Under the "IntrS" column, the amount in U.S. dollars per $100,000 sell position is provided.

TIME

Every time an exchange rate is changed, a time stamp is placed next to the currency pair. "Time" is recorded in Eastern Standard Time (EST) in the United States. A time stamp of 14:00 would mean that the last update occurred at 2:00 P.M. EST.

HIGHLIGHTING

In the Dealing Rates window, one of the rows will be underlined. The underlined currency pair will be the default currency pair when the trader enters market and entry orders. To change the underlined currency, click on the gray box directly to the left of the currency identification.

OPEN POSITIONS WINDOW

Figure 13-2 shows the Open Positions window.

TICKET AND ACCOUNT ID

Each row in the Open Positions window contains information about a specific open position. In the "Ticket" column there is a unique ticket number that enables the trader to track each position easily. The "Account ID" column is next and should be the same on each row.

CURRENCY, B/S, AMOUNT K, OPEN

Each open position has four major characteristics: (1) "Currency" (see "Currency" under "Dealing Rates Window" for an explanations), (2) "B/S" (see "Sell and Buy" under "Dealing Rates Window" for explanations), (3) "Amt K," the size of a position in increments of 100,000 of the base currency, and (4) "Open," the exchange rate at which the positions were opened. For example, a row that reads "EUR/USD, S, 500, 0.9220" means that the trader sold 500,000 euros for U.S. dollars at an exchange rate of 0.9220.

CLOSE

The "Close" column lists the current exchange rate at which the trader can exit the position. (For information on how to close a position, see "Close an Open Position" below.)

STOP AND LIMIT

The "Stop" and "Limit" columns allow stop-loss and limit orders to be placed on individual positions. A stop-loss order is used to prevent further

FIGURE 13-2 Open Position

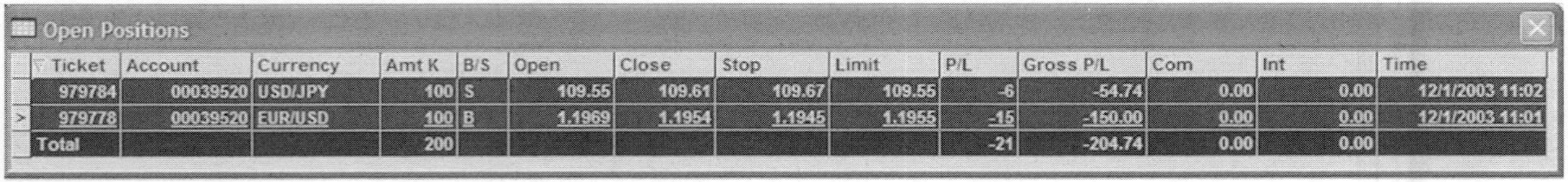

Open Positions

Ticket	Account	Currency	Amt K	B/S	Open	Close	Stop	Limit	P/L	Gross P/L	Com	Int	Time
979784	00039520	USD/JPY	100	S	109.55	109.61	109.67	109.55	-6	-54.74	0.00	0.00	12/1/2003 11:02
979778	00039520	EUR/USD	100	B	1.1969	1.1954	1.1945	1.1955	-15	-150.00	0.00	0.00	12/1/2003 11:01
Total			200						-21	-204.74	0.00	0.00	0.00

losses on a position after the exchange rate breaks through a prespecified level. The position will be liquidated at the next market price.

A limit order is used to lock in profits when the exchange rate hits a prespecified rate. These orders are only active for as long as the position remains open. For example, if a position has both a stop and a limit order on it and the limit order is triggered, the stop-loss order will be canceled.

P/L AND GROSS P/L

The profit/loss on each position is tracked in real time in both pips and U.S. dollars in the "P/L" and "Gross P/L" columns. Pips are calculated in the "P/L" column by multiplying the difference in pips between the open and close prices by the size of the trade. The profit/loss in U.S. dollars is shown in the "Gross P/L" column. A minus in front of the numbers in the "P/L" and "Gross P/L" columns indicates that the position has lost value.

COMMISSIONS

PremiereTrade does not charge any commissions.

INTEREST

This is the cumulative dollar amount that is added to or subtracted from an open position as a result of a rollover.

TIME

Each position bears a time stamp indicating when the position was opened.

HIGHLIGHTING

In the Open Positions window, one of the rows will be underlined. The highlighted position will be the default position when you enter orders to close or S/L. To change the highlighted position, click on the gray box on the far left of the row.

ACCOUNTS WINDOW

Figure 13-3 shows the Accounts window.

ACCOUNT

All account information is updated on a tick-by-tick basis in The "Account" column, giving traders a comprehensive view of their account. Each account has a unique ID. If a trader has multiple accounts—for example, a

FIGURE 13-3 Accounts

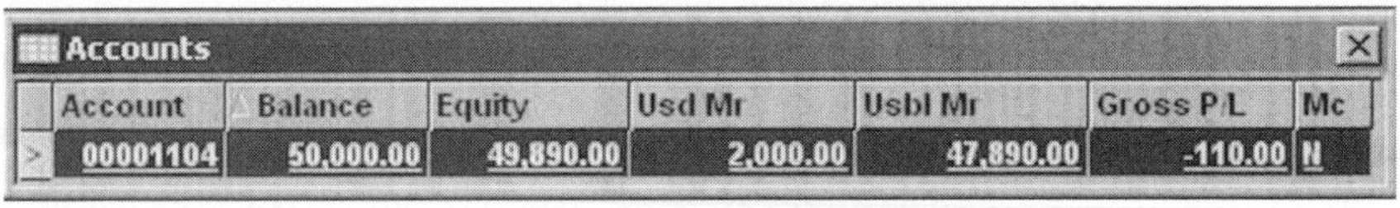

Account	Balance	Equity	Usd Mr	Usbl Mr	Gross P/L	Mc
00001104	50,000.00	49,890.00	2,000.00	47,890.00	-110.00	N

trader manages funds on behalf of several individuals—the trader will have multiple account IDs. The information for each account is maintained in a separate row.

BALANCE
The "Balance" column shows the value of funds in the account without taking into consideration profits and losses on open positions. The account balance is updated in real time.

EQUITY
The "Equity" column shows the value of funds in the account including profits and losses on open positions. The account equity also is updated in real time.

USD MR (USED MARGIN)
The "Usd Mr" column shows the amount of account equity currently being committed to maintain open positions. The trader must maintain $1000 for each $100,000 position. For example, if a trader has $500,000 in open positions, he or she would have $5000 in used margin. The used margin also is updated in real time.

USBL MR (USABLE MARGIN)
The "Usbl Mr" column shows the amount of account equity that is not currently being committed to maintain open positions. The formula for calculating usable margin is the account equity minus the used margin. The usable margin also is updated in real time.

MC (MARGIN CALL)
In the "Mc" column there will be a Y (yes) or an N (no). If Y appears, the usable margin reached zero, and open positions in the account were closed because there were insufficient funds. Please note that if this occurs, dealers have discretion over which open positions in the account will be closed.

MULTIPLE-ACCOUNTS WINDOW

For traders who have multiple accounts and wish to see them all at once, the trading software allows the trader simply to right click and highlight the account he or she wishes to view, and the trader will be able to see the Orders, Open Positions, and Summary windows in addition to the regular windows he or she can view from the main account. Figure 13-4 shows the Accounts window when there are multiple accounts.

ORDERS WINDOW

Figure 13-5 shows the Orders window.

ORDR ID (ORDER ID)

Each row in the Orders window contains information about a specific active entry order. The "Ordr ID" column lists a unique order ID that enables the trader to track each entry order easily.

T (TYPE)

The "T" column shows the type of order, of which there are two: (1) limit entry and (2) stop entry. If "LE" appears in the "T" column, the order is a limit entry. When placing a limit-entry order, a trader expects the exchange rate to move to a prespecified level and reverse direction. The limit-entry order will be executed if the exchange rate touches the prespecified level.

FIGURE 13-4   Account Reports

Account	Balance	Equity	Usd Mr	Usbl Mr	Gross P/L	Mc
99999999	1,038,622.85	1,038,542.85	1,000.00	1,037,542.85	-80.00	N
00009135	1,000.00	1,000.00	0.00	1,000.00	0.00	N
00000005	8,951.00	8,951.00	0.00	8,951.00	0.00	N

Reports
Show details

FIGURE 13-5   Orders

OrdrID	Account	T	Status	Currency	Sell	Buy	Amt K	Stop	Limit	Time
8786	0001104	LE	Waiting	GBP/USD	1.5578		100			10/31/2002 13:50

If "O" appears in the "T" column, the order is a stop entry. When placing a stop-entry order, a trader expects that if the exchange rate breaks through its prespecified level, it will continue to move in the same direction. The stop-entry order will be executed if the exchange rate breaks through the prespecified level.

CURRENCY, RATE, AMOUNT K, B/S

Each entry order has four major characteristics: (1) "Currency" (see "Currency" under the "Dealing Rates Window" for an explanations), (2) "Rate," which is the exchange rate that must be touched (limit entry) or broken through (stop entry) for the order to be executed, (3) "Sell" and "Buy" (see "Sell and Buy" under "Dealing Rates Window" for explanations), and (4) "Amt K" (amount K), the size of the position in increments of 100,000 of the base currency.

STOP AND LIMIT

The "Stop" and "Limit" columns that appear in the Orders window are nonactive orders until the entry order is executed. The entry order will then disappear from the Orders Window and appear in the Open Positions window with the stop and limit orders becoming active.

TIME

Each order bears a time stamp indicating when it was placed.

HIGHLIGHTING

In the Orders window, one of the rows will be underlined. The underlined position will be the default position when you enter orders to close or enter Stop/Limit orders. To change the Underlined position, click on the gray box at the far left of the row.

PLACING A MARKET ORDER

There are four different ways to open the "Market Order" box:

1.   In the Dealing Rates window, click on the exchange rate for the desired currency and operation (buy or sell).
2.   Right click on the appropriate rate and select the "Market Order" command from the pop-up menu that appears.
3.   Click on the "Buy" button at the top of the trading screen, which causes the "Market Order" box to appear.

4.   Click on the "Action" heading located at the top of the screen above the "Quote" button. From there, select "Dealing Rates" and then "Market Orders."

Figure 13-6 shows the "Market Order" box.

"MARKET ORDER" BOX

There are five parameters a trader can set prior to sending an order to the trading desk:

Account. If the trader has more than one account, clicking on the "Account" option will enable the trader to select the account from which the trades will be placed.

Currency. The "Currency" will default automatically to the currency pairing that is highlighted in the Dealing Rates window. However, any pairing can be selected simply by scrolling down the list of currencies.

Buy/Sell. This command will either buy or sell the first currency listed. The command will default to either "Buy" or "Sell" depending on how the user summons up the pop-up menu. Left clicking on the "Dealing Rate" or clicking the "Buy" or "Sell" button will prompt the default. Right clicking on the "Dealing

FIGURE 13-6   Market Order

Rate" or clicking on the "Action" heading will not automatically set the default to the operation desired.

Amount. Trades are made in increments of 100,000 of the base currency.

Rate. This is the rate at which the trade will be executed, and the trader cannot change this.

At Market Feature

This feature enables clients to customize the range of rates they are willing to accept; orders simply will be executed at the first rate the market reaches that is within the range specified by the trader, thus ensuring rapid execution and the ability to create and liquidate positions easily.

Stops/Limits

This command will allow the trader to select the exchange rate at which the stop or limit should be triggered. The rate defaults automatically to 5 pips away from the current relevant market rate for both stop and limit orders. However, a trader can click on the box to the right of the "Rate" option and enter a specific rate for his or her stop/limit order.

At any time during the stop/limit input process, a trader can cancel the order by clicking on the "Cancel" button. Click on the "New" button after all the selections have been made to place the stop/limit order. Once the order is placed, the information will be updated under the "Stop" or "Limit" box in the Open Positions window.

COMPLETING THE TRADE

At any time during the trade input process, a trader can cancel the order by clicking the "Cancel" button. Click on the "OK" button after all the selections have been made to execute the trade.

After "OK" has been selected, one of the following two responses will occur:

- The trade order will be displayed in the Open Positions window.

- A box will appear indicating that you do not have enough funds in your account for the transaction.

When the trade appears in the Open Positions window, this confirms that the order has been executed. *Note:* Opening a new position (buy EUR/sell USD) that is the opposite and in the same amount as an existing open position (buy USD/sell EUR) will effectively close the original position and serve to cancel the other position out.

PLACING A STOP/LIMIT ON AN OPEN POSITION

There are four different ways to open the "Stop/Limit Order" box:

1.   In the Open Positions window, click on either the "Stop" or "Limit" box of the highlighted ticket you wish to update.

2.   Right click on the appropriate "Stop" or "Limit" box from the highlighted ticket and select the "Stop Order" command from the pop-up menu.

3.   Click on the "Stop/Limit" button at the top of the trading screen, which causes the "Stop/Limit Order" box to appear.

4.   Click on the "Action" heading located on the top of the screen above the "Quote" button. From there, select "Positions" and then "Stop/Limit."

Figure 13-7 shows the "Stop Order" and "Limit Order" boxes.

"STOP/LIMIT ORDER" BOX

There are three parameters a trader can set prior to sending an order to the trading desk:

Ticket. Select the specific ticket number of the ticket on which the stop or limit will be placed. The "Ticket" option will default automatically to whichever ticket is highlighted in the Open Positions window. However, any ticket can be selected simply by scrolling down the list of numbers and clicking on the correct number.

Stop/Limit. This command will allow the trader to place either a stop or a limit order on the selected ticket.

Rate. This command will allow the trader to select the exchange rate at which the stop or limit should be triggered. The rate defaults automatically to 5 pips below the current sell rate for stop orders and 5 pips above the current sell rate for limit orders. However, the trader can click on the box to the right of the "Rate" option and enter a specific rate for his or her stop/limit order.

At any time during the stop/limit input process, a trader can cancel the order by clicking on the "Cancel" button. Click on the "New" button after all the selections have been made to place the stop/limit order. Once the order is placed, the information will be updated under the "Stop" or "Limit" box in the Open Positions window.

FIGURE 13-7   Stop/Limit Orders

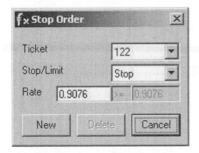 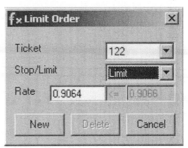

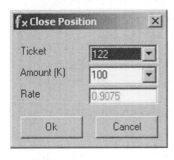

FIGURE 13-8   Close Position

CHANGE PRICE ON A STOP/LIMIT (OPEN POSITION)

To change the price for an existing stop/limit order on an open position, the trader must click on the "Rate" option in the "Stop Order" box and enter the new rate for the specific ticket number. The trader can bring up the "Stop Order" box four different ways as explained under "Placing a Stop/Limit on an Open Position" above. The trader can then click "Okay," and the new rate should be updated in the appropriate "Stop" or "Limit" box in the "Open Positions" window.

DELETE STOP/LIMIT (OPEN POSITION)

To delete an existing stop/limit order on an open position, the trader must click on the "Delete" button in the "Stop Order" box for the specific ticket number. The trader can bring up the "Stop Order" box in the four different ways as explained under "Placing a Stop/Limit on an Open Position" above. Once the trader deletes the existing stop/limit order, the applicable "Stop" or "Limit" box in the Open Positions window will be empty.

CLOSE AN OPEN POSITION

There are four different ways to open the "Close Position" box:

1. In the Open Positions window, click on the "Close" box of the highlighted ticket the trader wishes to close. This will cause the "Close Position" box to pop up and allow the trader to close the position.
2. The trader also can right click on the "Close" box from the highlighted ticket and select the "Close Position" command from the pop-up menu. Once again, the "Close Position" box will appear, allowing the trader to close the position.
3. The trader also can close out a position by clicking on the "Close" button at the top of the trading screen. Again, this will prompt the "Close Position" box to appear.
4. The same menu also will appear by left clicking the "Action" option (above the "Quote" button) at the very top of the screen. From there, select "Positions" and then "Close Position."

Figure 13-8 shows the "Close Position" box.

"CLOSE POSITION" BOX

There are two parameters that a trader can set prior to sending the close to the trading desk:

Ticket. Select the specific ticket number that is to be closed. The "Ticket" option will default automatically to whichever ticket is highlighted in the Open Positions window. However, any ticket can be selected simply by scrolling down the list of numbers and clicking on the correct number.

Amount. Select the dollar amount to be closed. The "Amount" option automatically selects all dollars to be closed out. However, any amount can be selected simply by scrolling down the list of dollar figures.

At any time during the close position process, a trader can cancel the order by clicking on the "Cancel" button. Once the position is closed, it will disappear from the Open Positions window. Click on the "OK" button after

FIGURE 13-9   Entry Orders

all the selections have been made to close the position. Once the order is completed, the account balance will be adjusted in the Account Information window.

PLACING AN ENTRY ORDER

There are three ways to open the "Entry Order" box:

1. In the Orders window, right click on any part of the window and select the "Create Entry Order" command from the pop-up menu. The "Entry Order" box will appear, allowing the trader to place the order.

2. An entry order also can be placed by left clicking on the "Entry" button at the top of the trading screen. This will prompt the "Entry Order" box to appear and allow the trader to place the order.

3. The same menu also will appear by left clicking the "Action" option (above the "Quote" button) at the very top of the screen. From there, select "Orders" and then "Create Entry Order."

    Figure 13-9 shows the "Entry Order" box.

"ENTRY ORDER" BOX

There are five parameters a trader can set prior to sending an order to the trading desk. The first four are the same ones that appear in the "Market

Order" box (account, currency, buy/sell, and amount). However, the difference is that for an entry order the trader sets a specific level to trigger execution of the trade. An entry order remains active until either the trade is executed or the trader cancels it.

At any time during the trade input process, a trader can cancel the order by clicking the "Cancel" button. Click on the "OK" button after all the selections have been made to execute the trade. Once the order is accepted, the information will be listed in the Orders window. Once the trade is executed, the position will disappear from the Orders window and reappear as an open position in the Open Positions window.

CHANGE AN ENTRY ORDER

There are four ways to open the "Change Order Rate" box (*Note:* The "Order ID" automatically defaults to the highlighted order in the "Order Entry" box):

1.   In the Orders window, click on the "Rate" box of the highlighted order or the order the trader wishes to update. This will cause the "Change Order Rate" box to pop up and allow the trader to change the order.

2.   In the Orders window, right click on any part of the window and select the "Change Entry Order" command from the pop-up menu. The "Change Order Rate" box will appear, allowing the trader to change the order.

3.   A change to an entry order also can be made by left clicking on the "Change" button at the top of the trading screen. Again, this will prompt the "Change Order Rate" box to appear.

4.   The same box also will appear by left clicking the "Action" option (above the "Quote" button) at the very top of the screen. From there, select "Orders" and then "Change Entry Order."

FIGURE 13-10   Change Order Rate

Figure 13-10 shows the "Change Order Rate" box.

"CHANGE ORDER RATE" BOX

There are two parameters a trader can set prior to sending an order to the trading desk:

Order ID. If the trader has several pending entry positions, select the specific order number of the order that is going to be changed. The "Order ID" option will default automatically to whichever order is highlighted in the Orders window. However, any order can be selected simply by scrolling down the list of numbers and clicking on the correct number.

Rate. This option allows the trader to select the new exchange rate at which the entry order should be triggered. The trader clicks on the box to the right of the "Rate" option and enters a specific rate for the selected entry order.

At any time during the order change process, the trader can cancel the changes by clicking the "Cancel" button. Click on the "OK" button after all the selections have been made. Once the trade is completed, the updated information will be listed in the Orders window.

Only the exchange rate can be changed for an existing entry order. The dollar amount or currency selection cannot be changed for any particular

FIGURE 13-11 Advance/Simple Dealing Rates

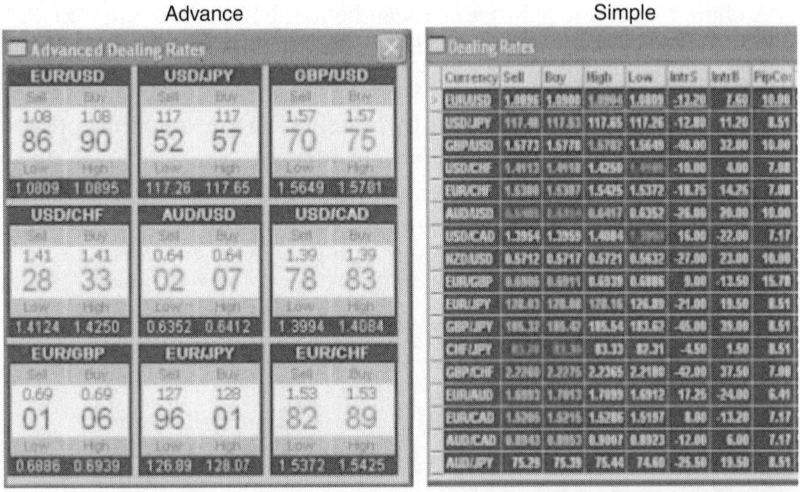

"Order ID" number. The user must input a new entry order and remove the existing one to effect changes in amount and currency.

CANCELING AN ENTRY ORDER

There are two ways to open the "Delete Order" box:

1. In the Orders window, right click on any part of the window and select the "Remove Order" command from the pop-up menu. The "Delete Order" box will appear, allowing the trader to delete the trade.
2. The "Remove Order" menu also will appear by left clicking the "Action" option (above the "Quote" button) at the very top of the screen. From there, select "Orders" and then "Remove Order."

"DELETE ORDER" BOX

The trader will be asked if the highlighted order ID number is to be deleted. Click "Yes" to cancel the trade, and click "No" to make no changes to the order. Once the "Yes" button is clicked, the order will be deleted from the Orders window and officially removed.

REPORTS

To access this feature, click on the "Reports" button located at the top of the screen, and select the time period of interest. Traders can pull up a detailed report of their account status on a daily, weekly, monthly, or yearly basis. This report presents, in a format ideal for printing, such key account information as records of floating positions and completed trades.

CUSTOMIZING THE TRADING SCREEN

Each window can be customized to meet a trader's personal specifications. There are several modifications that can be made.

SHOW OR HIDE WINDOW SCREENS

To show or hide any of the four window screens (Accounts, Dealing Rates, Open Positions, Entry Orders), simply click on the boxes located at the top of the trading screen. To hide a screen, a trader also may click on the "X" box in the upper right-hand corner of the window.

CHANGE WINDOW SIZE

To move a window or adjust the window size, follow the same procedures you would use for any Windows-based program. Simply click on the outer edge of the window and drag it to the size desired.

ADJUSTING BOX SIZES INSIDE A WINDOW

To adjust the individual box sizes inside each window, simply click on the outer edge of the box and drag it to the left or right to the desired size.

SELECTING THE CURRENCY PAIRS FOR THE DEALING RATES WINDOW

The trader has the option of adding or removing currency pairings to and from the Dealing Rates window. To do this, the trader must open the "Currency Subscribe List" box. There are two ways to open this box:

1.   In the Dealing Rates window, right click on any part of the window, and select the "Currency Subscribe List" command from the pop-up menu. The "Currency Subscribe List" box will appear, allowing the trader to choose which currency pairings he or she wishes to view.

2.   The "Currency Subscribe List" menu also will appear by clicking the "Action" option (above the "Quote" button) at the very top of the screen. From there, select "Dealing Rates" and then "Currency Subscribe List."

CHANGING THE LOOK AND FEEL

A trader can either choose a simple or advanced look. To change the look of the Dealing Rates window, left click on "Action," then "Dealing Rates," and then "Look & Feel." There are two selections: "Advanced Dealing Rates" and "Dealing Rates" (see Figure 13-11).

OPTIONS CURRENCY SUBSCRIBE LIST BOX

A trader can either add or remove a currency pair from among the 17 currency pairings that the trading platform offers. *Note:* Once an order is placed or a position is opened, the trader will be unable to unsubscribe from any currency pairings until all positions are closed or removed.

To add a currency pairing, simply highlight the pairing and then click the "Subscribe" button. The pairing will then show up in the Dealing Rates window, and there will be a "T" in the "Status" column inside the "Currency Subscribe List" box.

FIGURE 13-12   Options

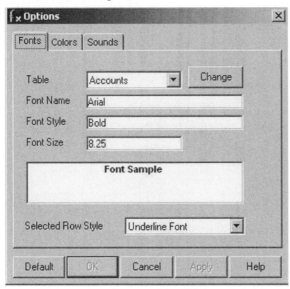

To remove a currency pairing, simply highlight the pairing and then click the "Unsubscribe" button. The pairing will then show up in the Dealing Rates window, and there will be a "D" in the "Status" column inside the "Currency Subscribe List" box.

TRADING STATION OPTIONS

There are some additional features that allow traders to customize their platform when it comes to font size, color, and sound. They are listed below.

FONT SIZE

To change the font size of the characters inside each window, click on "File," "Options," and then "Font." Highlight the window you wish to change the fonts for in the "Table" box, and then click the "Change" button.

A "Font" box will appear that will allow you to change the font type, style, and size of the characters for that window. Click the "OK" button after the changes have been made, and the desired font will be updated inside that window. Figure 13-12 shows the "Options" box for changing the font sizes for a window.

The font size also may be changed by clicking on the "Action" heading located at the top of the screen above the "Quote" button. From there, select

FIGURE 13-13   Color Options

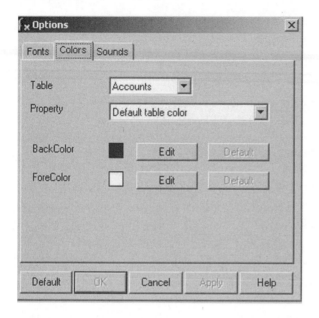

either "Accounts," "Dealing Rates," "Orders," or "Positions," and then click on "Font" to change the font for the chosen window.

COLORS

To change the color of the characters inside each window, click on "File," "Options," and "Colors." Highlight the window for which you wish to change colors in the "Table" box, and then click the "Change" button.

A "Color" box will appear that will allow you to change the color of the characters for that window. Click the "OK" button after the changes have been made, and the desired color will be updated inside that window. Figure 13-13 shows the "Options" box for changing colors.

SOUND

The sound feature allows the client to program the software to make a sound for a variety to differentiate various functions from an update in the dealing rates to a margin call. To use this function (or to silence it), click on "File," "Options," and then "Sounds," which will allow you to make your choices. Figure 13-14 shows the "Options" box for sound changes.

FIGURE 13-14   Sound Options

FIGURE 13-15   Select Interface Language

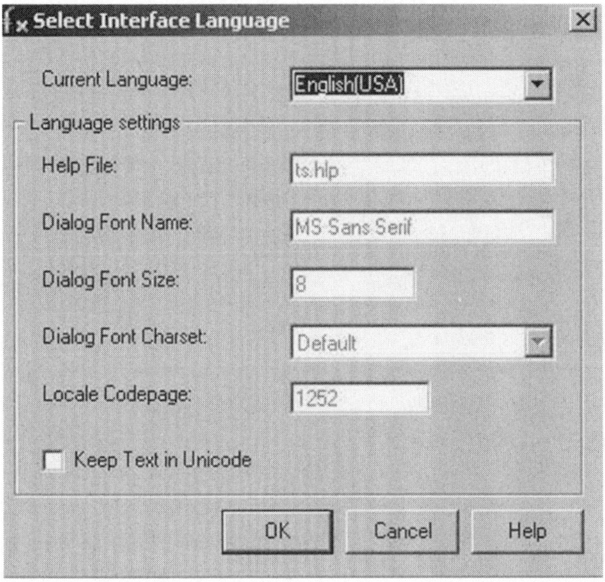

SELECT INTERFACE LANGUAGE

To change the language on the trading station, click on "File," "Language," and then select the language in which you wish to view the platform. Once you have selected the language, you must restart the trading station for the change to take effect. See Figure 13-15.

By becoming familiar with the trade station, you will have a much better opportunity at making profitable trades. As you explore the trade station using a demo account, you will start to become efficient at the functions detailed in this chapter. The trade station is very user friendly and very easy to use.

14

CORPORATIONS IN THE FOREX

- Introduction
- Forward Transactions
- Examples of Strategies
- Portfolio Management and Currency Risk

INTRODUCTION

Recognition of the financial risks associated with the foreign exchange market (FOREX) means that some decisions need to be made. The key to any good management is a rational approach to decision making.

The most desirable method of management is the preplanning of responses to movements in what are generally volatile markets so that emotions are dispensed with and previous careful planning is relied on. This approach helps to eliminate the panic factor because all outcomes have been considered, including worst-case scenarios, which could result from either action or inaction.

Even though the worst-case scenarios are considered and plans ensure that even such worst-case scenarios are acceptable (although not desirable), the preplanning focuses on achieving the best result.

Corporations doing business internationally have had to deal with the economic consequences of fluctuations in floating exchange rates. Whether large or small, for corporations that have outstanding contracts internationally with buyers, sellers, or manufacturers, transactional risk is becoming a huge concern. For example, Caterpillar in 1986 posted a $76 million profit after a $24 million operational loss. These profits were the result of a $100 million profit from foreign exchange.

Many orders for products or services are agreed on well in advance, along with future currency values. During the negotiations, prices are always set. However, it is equally important to protect these contracts from exposure to free-floating currency. For example, in June, a U.S. corporation enters into a contract with a corporation in Japan. Japan will manufacture a product for a price of 1.2 million yen, which works out to $10,000 with the USD/JPY currently trading at 120.00.

1.2 million yen ÷ 120.00 = $10,000 (price agreed on by both parties)

In 6 months, that currency pair could be trading at the same price of 120.00, but more likely, the price will not stay the same as currencies continuously change.

Let's take a look at how the U.S. corporation would be affected if the pair were trading at 100.00 or 140.00:

1.2 million yen ÷ 100.00 = $12,000 (cost increases for U.S. corporation)

1.2 million yen ÷ 140.00 = $8571 (cost decreased for U.S. corporation)

As these examples show, fluctuation of currencies can have a positive or negative effect. The proliferation of risk-management tools, the extraordinary volume of literature that is published on the subject, and the focusing of academic attention on improving risk-management techniques all point to the importance of risk management as a key management issue.

Active risk management is a common characteristic in by far the majority of major corporations the world over. Not to manage financial risk is seen to be negligent because a company's management team is responsible for managing all the variables that ultimately affect the profitability of the company.

FORWARD TRANSACTIONS

While profit can turn into losses quickly, corporations have found it mandatory to enter into forward transactions, such as futures, swaps, and options.

FUTURES

Foreign currency *futures* are forward transactions. These transactions have standard contract sizes and maturity dates, for example, 1 million Japanese yen for next January at an agreed-on rate. These contracts are traded on a separate exchange set up for that purpose.

SWAPS

The most common type of forward transaction among corporations is the currency *swap*. In a swap, two parties exchange currencies for a certain length of time and agree to reverse the transaction at a later date. This will offset both corporations from exposure to the fluctuating market.

OPTIONS

Currency *options* can efficiently lower a corporation's currency risk because they are custom tailored to the specifications of the corporation. The corporation is able to determine the amount of currency being hedged, the length of the option, and the degree of exposure to market fluctuations.

A currency option is an insurance policy for a corporation in which it determines the deductible, length of the policy, and coverage. The advantages of hedging with options include

- Currency risk exposure is limited to predetermined amounts.

- The potential for profit from currency market fluctuations is not limited.

- Only minimal cash outlays are required in relation to other hedging methods.

EXAMPLES OF STRATEGIES

SCALED-IN SELLING

This is a very simple strategy, and it is also particularly successful. It normally involves the estimation of a range that the relevant currency will trade in over the period of the exposure.

When an importer needs to purchase U.S. dollars, he or she would seek to buy the dollars when the AUD/USD exchange rate is at its highest. Assume that the current exchange rate is 0.6300 and that it is felt that the AUD/USD is likely to trade at between 0.6250 and 0.6600 during the life of the exposure. In this case the importer would set up a strategy such as the following:

At 0.6400, purchase 20 percent of requirements.

At 0.6450, purchase 20 percent of requirements.

At 0.6500, purchase 20 percent of requirements.

At 0.6550, purchase 20 percent of requirements.

At 0.6600, purchase 20 percent of requirements.

In this way, an average rate of 0.6500 is achieved instead of the prevailing spot rate of 0.6300. However, if the view turns out to be incorrect, then the worst-case trigger is touched, and the exposure is covered at 0.6245, just outside the expected range. This is only 55 pips worse than covering at the then-spot rate. If the best case is achieved, then you have done better by 200 pips.

TAKING OUT "INSURANCE"

This type of strategy employs foreign exchange options, which are widely used products. Let's look at the case of a corporation that suffers when the AUD loses value. If that corporation were to buy an option that would protect it from downward movements in the AUD but still left it with the opportunity to benefit if the AUD were to gain strength, then this would appear to be a good, safe strategy, and in fact, it is.

Options are just like insurance. They protect against worst-case scenarios while still leaving room to benefit when things are favorable.

WORKING AN EXPOSURE

This is a fairly aggressive strategy in which a business unit hedges and non-hedges the exposure to take advantage of a market that is range trading and seems to have no real direction. For example, if the business unit hedges the exposure at 0.6500 and the AUD/USD rate subsequently falls to 0.6300, the business unit could take a profit of 200 pips.

Assuming that the rates were just range trading and went back up, the business unit could put on the hedge again at 0.6500, and because of the 200-pip profit, it achieve an average rate of 0.6700. This may happen a number of times, and extraordinarily effective rates of exchange may be achieved.

It sounds risky, but a worst-case plan can easily guard against the situation where the AUD starts to depreciate rapidly. For example, the exposure is fully covered if it breaks lower than 0.6250. At this time the corporate may already have 400 pips up its sleeve.

The number of different strategies available is only limited by the imagination and the skill of the planner. It is not difficult to formulate these strategies with the right advice, and it is certainly not difficult to implement them.

PORTFOLIO MANAGEMENT AND CURRENCY RISK

Fund managers have different foreign exchange requirements than corporations because foreign exchange exposures occur as a result of investment activities as opposed to trade activities. Fund managers are often working within a benchmarked framework, and managing foreign exchange risks incorrectly can give rise to unwanted and unexpected deviation on returns, even when they are trying to stay at benchmark.

Fund managers should be aware of not only the benchmarks set for them but also how to manage to the benchmark return. This is often more complex than may first appear because benchmark indices are set periodically, and fund size changes can affect the currency weighting in unexpected ways.

FULLY HEDGED PORTFOLIOS

Most fund managers run international bond portfolios fully hedged, which means that for every foreign bond exposure, they have a corresponding hedge in place. Usually the hedge takes the form of a forward sale of foreign currency for, say, Australian dollars normally on a rolling 3-month basis.

In practical terms, this means that on purchasing a foreign bond, the fund manager should enter a swap or forward (FX) contract. This means that on the near leg of the swap, the manager can buy the foreign currency against AUD (to pay for the bond), and the second leg is for the sale of the foreign currency against the AUD and neutralizes the forward risk.

An example would be a fund manager executing a spot to buy the foreign currency and then an outright deal to sell the foreign currency forward. The net effect is the same as a swap, except that the fund pays an unnecessary spread in the spot market.

Once the hedges are due for settlement, the fund simply executes another swap. The near leg is equal and opposite to the maturing deals (except that the rate is now the current spot), and the second leg reinstates the forward hedge.

The portfolio manager also needs to decide which currency to keep constant—Australian dollars or the foreign currency. In general, it is the foreign currency that should be kept constant in line with the value of the bond holdings.

If the foreign currency hedge amount is kept constant, be aware that each roll date will give rise to an AUD profit or loss on the hedge. Also, at each roll date the value of the foreign bond needs to be taken into account and the hedge adjusted accordingly to make sure that the portfolio is not over- or underhedged.

NONHEDGED PORTFOLIOS

When a fund manager is running a portfolio nonhedged, then foreign currency should be bought and sold as needed to satisfy the underlying transaction. These transactions should be executed when the underlying assets are purchased or sold and have value dates matching the settlement terms of the underlying asset.

Foreign currency is the key to the economic stability of all governments and countries. As long as governments and corporations do business with each other across the world, foreign currency transactions will be prevalent. Every transaction will have a positive and a negative just as if you or I were trading the currency.

15

THE BUSINESS
OF TRADING

- Starting Your Business
- The Tax Code
- How to Become a Trader
- What If I Don't Make Enough Money to Use Those Deductions?
- How to Make the Win/Win Better
- What Kind of Corporation Should You Use?
- Let's Take a Look at Some Examples

STARTING YOUR BUSINESS

Now that you are a trader, you should always be on the lookout for ways to increase your returns. In addition to increasing the actual returns you make on trades, you also should look for ways your trading can make or save you money.

In reality, it doesn't matter where your income or profit comes from as long as your cash increases at the end of each month. This is what I refer to as the *business* of trading.

Most people don't think about trading as a business, but I learned long ago that the best returns frequently can be made by looking at things differently than most people. If you change your thinking and start looking at trading as more than just investing but actually as a business that provides income for you and your family, I think you will be pleasantly surprised at the benefits you receive.

In the first place, a small business is about the only great tax shelter still available that the Internal Revenue Service (IRS) hasn't been able to strip away. Not that it hasn't tried, but Congress has stubbornly realized that it is the entrepreneurial sprit that makes this country what it is, so it has consistently avoided reducing the benefits businesses offer to their owners.

Naturally, it doesn't hurt that most congresspersons and senators either have small businesses or relatives who have one, but let's be thankful for the little favors we get, no matter where they come from or what form they take.

THE TAX CODE

The tax code classifies people in the securities business into three categories: dealers, investors, and traders. The dealer classification is beyond the scope of this book because it involves people making a market in stocks and other securities for investors. Investors and traders, however, are very important and affect the way we buy and sell currencies or securities and what deductions we are allowed.

Most people consider themselves investors. They invest and look for a return on their money. Investors, however, do not get any tax benefits other than the potential of capital gain tax treatment on anything they buy and hold for more than a year.

In this market, holding anything for as long as a year may be a financial disaster; the benefit isn't all that great today, In fact, the jaded side of me wonders if the fact that it isn't really a benefit is the real reason Congress is thinking about doing away with the tax on capital gains.

If, instead of being an investor, you decide to be a trader, here is a partial list of benefits in the form of tax deductions you get:

- The cost of your trading education

- The cost of financial software

- The cost of books and audio/videotape courses in investing and trading

- Accounting fees

- Brokerage account fees and commissions

- The cost of office equipment (computers, Internet high-speed connection fees, adding machines, phones, phone charges, etc.)

- Interest on your margin accounts and any other investment-related interest expense

- The cost of financial advice and training

- The cost of tax advice

- The cost of legal advice related to your business

- Entertainment and meals expenses during which business is conducted

- The cost of travel to seminars, trade shows, and other business-related trips, anywhere in the world

- The cost of magazine subscriptions related to investing and trading

- The cost of trips to look at corporations in which you are considering investing

- The portion of your home expense that qualifies as a home business and a portion of all expenses paid on maintaining the property

- Automobile expenses

You can tell that the list is rather inclusive and beneficial. Interestingly, as you begin to learn the nuances and combine all the advantages, they add up to a rather tidy sum. For example, if the year you become a trader you purchase a new car to be used in your business, you can take an immediate deduction for the first $25,000 because the car qualifies under Section 29 of the tax code, which allows for asset expensing of the first $25,000 of property bought for use in your business each year.

The rest of the cost of the car can be set up on a depreciation schedule for future years. It isn't a reason to go out and buy a new car (or is it?), but it isn't bad.

HOW TO BECOME A TRADER

The IRS code does not define trade or business as it relates to the business of trading. The law that has developed comes from court cases and decisions made in the favor of taxpayers who have made this claim. The key elements in the cases were length of holding period, frequency of trades, and whether the person's activity was intent on making the money from dividend interest, long-term gains, or profits from short-term trading.

If you are a currency trader, it is pretty easy to show your intent because this is all you shoot for. If you also trade stocks, you can still make a claim for trader status even if you hold some of them long term, although it is doubtful you will anyway.

WHAT IF I DON'T MAKE ENOUGH MONEY TO USE THOSE DEDUCTIONS?

While we all hope our businesses, including our trading business, makes a ton of money, the reality is it won't always do so. The good news is that if trading is a business, then your excess expenses can be used to offset income from other sources, just like any other business would allow you to do. It is a win/win situation.

HOW TO MAKE THE WIN/WIN BETTER

So far I have talked about using trader status as it relates to your personal tax return by creating a small sole proprietorship. In this case you would place your ordinary business expenses on Schedule C, and you would report your income or loss on Schedule D because it is still considered capital. No self-employment income is calculated on the income, and your trading losses are still limited to $3000 per year but can be carried over indefinitely. You also can use any losses in the stock market to offset gains in the currency market.

Although the benefits of this strategy are good, there is another way—and in many ways, a better way—to operate the business. This is by incorporating the business and creating your own trade corporation.

A trade corporation is your new legal entity in which to conduct your trading. There are near-term advantages, longer-range asset protection, and family financial planning advantages. There will be some extra cost for setup and operation, but as you will quickly see, the advantages far outweigh the cost.

Your first advantage is clarity of purpose. If you form a corporation for the purpose of trading and conduct the trading in that separate entity, there will be no question regarding your trader status, nor an issue about your personal tax return and the deductions you take. This is not to suggest that operating things in the sole proprietorship status is in the gray area of the tax code. It isn't.

Some people like to keep their various businesses separate, protect assets from different creditors, and do estate and financial planning as they go. If you fall into this category of individuals, you should consider using a corporation as the entity to operate your trade business.

WHAT KIND OF CORPORATION SHOULD YOU USE?

There are three types of corporations: a *C Corporation,* which is considered a regular corporation; a *Sub S Corporation,* so named because of the tax code section that gives it benefits, and the *Limited-Liability Corporation* (LLC), which is a relatively new corporate structured to overcome some of the structural difficulties of the Sub S Corporation. (Interestingly, about the time the states got through adopting all this massive legislation to get around the tax code, Congress decided that it didn't want to be outdone and amended most, but not all, of the difficult portions of the Sub S code.)

To be fair to both you as the reader and me as the author, I must now disclose that I am going to make sweeping generalities about which corporations are best and why. The problem is that everyone's circumstances are different, and volumes have been written about the "best" structure to use. Nevertheless, I will attempt to weed through the jargon of red tape and see if some meat comes forth.

The C Corporation is used primarily for public companies, multiple shareholders who aren't interested in distributing profits and losses but want to build an entity, and individual businesses that want to benefit from a medical reimbursement plan and/or some types of retirement programs. For some people, the medical reimbursement can be a great deal because under the current law individuals and joint filers are limited to medical deductions after a 2 percent limitation of adjusted gross income.

If you make $150,000 per year adjusted gross income, you can only deduct medical expenses above $3000. If, on the other hand, you have a C Corporation and you have adopted a medical reimbursement plan, you would be able to get a deduction from the first dollar, plus all of your family's expenses. It is a nice benefit if you need it.

Excepting the medical situation, you likely will benefit greatest in either a Sub S Corporation or an LLC. The reason is that both have tax flow benefits at the shareholder level. This means that the corporation does not pay a separate tax but that the shareholders (in the Sub S) and the members (in the LLC) pay tax on any gain or take losses personally if there are any. This gives you the benefit of a personal tax shelter in years there is a loss in the company.

The benefit to using a Sub S structure is that it has been around the longest and most certified public accountants (CPAs) and attorneys are comfortable with it. The benefit of the LLC is that you can do some interesting family, estate, and asset-protection planning.

LET'S TAKE A LOOK AT SOME EXAMPLES

You form an LLC trade corporation. In an LLC, you are allowed to issue multiple types of shares. Because you would like to shift some of your trade income to your children, you issue them a preferred class of stock that has no voting rights but has a preference of income up to a certain level.

This "income shift" strategy allows you to maintain 100 percent control of your company and all the assets but shift dollars to your children, who are in a lower income bracket than you. The children can use the money to pay their bills.

Another twist on this strategy is to pay your children a salary out of the corporation for work they do. The work, depending on age and ability, would give them earned income and allow them to set up an Individual Retirement Account (IRA) or other retirement program at an early age.

While income shifting takes money out of your pocket and puts it in someone else's, you get the deduction, and if you can control what happens to the money, it is the same as having it. Another benefit to helping your children grow an early retirement program is that you may at least have someone to support you if things don't always go as you would like.

LLCs have another advantage: They can be used to protect assets. If you find yourself in a situation where you need to be protected, you can put your assets in an LLC and give, sell, or otherwise structure the share ownership in someone else's name. You can continue to draw a salary from the company and control the operation of the company through special shares, which can be drafted to give you specific rights to do so.

The assets now belong to someone else and are no longer attachable by creditors, and the income you receive is not attachable because it is a salary. (Some states give certain creditors rights to lien a potion of salary, but this can be adjusted to fit the situation.) Please note that in this example you have actually given up these shares and the assets they represent. This can be a shame. On the other hand, in the scenario I outlined, you would have lost the assets to a creditor not of your choosing.

By using this structure you at least shifted the assets to someone you know, and you get income generated from the company in the form of a salary. I also would like to point out that there are laws governing fraud on creditors. These laws do not prevent you from properly protecting yourself and your family but are intend to stop what are called *sham transactions,* where there is no truth or substance to your actions. Since we are only talking about proper planning, these and other strategies should all be available to you and used when needed.

BRETTON WOODS SYSTEM AND POST–BRETTON WOODS SYSTEM

I n July 1944, in Bretton Woods, New Hampshire, representatives of 44 nations met to establish the standards by which international trade and finance would be conducted once World War II had ended. This included not only specification of the exchange rate and payments system that would prevail but also provisions for helping the third-world nations develop in the postcolonial era.

In its final form, the plan was something less than its primary architects, Harry Dexter White and John Maynard Keynes, had hoped. Nonetheless, the stability it lent to the postwar period helped create an environment conducive to recovery. However, the tranquility was not to last. In the end, it appears that the exchange rate and payments mechanism contained the seeds of its own destruction, allowing—even encouraging—developments to take place that led to its demise.

Meanwhile, many argue that the efforts to develop emerging economies have done more harm than good (Danaher 1994). From those events, especially the massive internationalization of capital, evolved the modern international monetary system.

Independently, White, in the United States, and Keynes, in Great Britain, had been developing ambitious plans for the postwar international economy since the early 1940s (Shelton 1994, pp. 24–28). Both had conceived of a system wherein exchange rate stability was a prime goal, and they shared an intense desire to engineer an arrangement that promoted cooperation and humanitarian goals. Neither of them favored a return to a classical gold standard.

The most significant difference between their approaches was that White's scheme tended to favor incentives designed to create price stability within the world's economies, whereas Keynes wanted a system that encouraged economic growth. In the end, though, true compromise was achieved on some points, and the overwhelming economic and military power of the United States led to the adoption of a largely American plan.

The international monetary system that emerged was a gold exchange standard. The U.S. dollar was fixed to gold and convertible on demand (at $35 per ounce). All other currencies were fixed to the dollar (and therefore to gold) and were allowed to fluctuate around that value only within a narrow band. Central banks were expected to intervene in the event that their home currency moved or threatened to move outside that band.

If a currency's value appeared to have permanently shifted well beyond the par rate, the country in question had the right under the articles of agreement to declare that a fundamental disequilibrium existed. The rules of the system were then supposed to allow that country some recourse (either revaluation or devaluation of its money).

In addition to these exchange rate–specific regulations, Bretton Woods also established a fund (the International Monetary Fund) from which countries could draw when facing temporary payment difficulties. At the same time, the World Bank was established to help integrate the less developed economies into the world capitalist economy. This was to be achieved through a combination of advice, direct loans, and guarantees of third-party loans.

The spectacular growth of the former combatants after the war is well known. Bretton Woods was certainly not the only reason for this "miracle," especially in light of the fact that not all of its provisions (in particular, the convertibility obligations) were in full force until 1958 and that the impact of U.S. policy, especially the Marshall Plan, was undoubtedly greater than that of the World Bank. Nonetheless, their stabilizing presence in this particularly unpredictable period must have encouraged international trade and investment. By the late 1960s, however, flaws in the exchange rate and payments system were becoming evident.

To begin, the par rates set after the war assumed an overwhelmingly dominant U.S. economy. At first, this proved an accurate assumption because the United States ran large balance-of-payments surpluses until 1950. However, as the European economies recovered, the U.S. payments balance slipped into deficit. This was relatively small until 1958, when it began to increase sharply.

Given the worldwide shortage of dollars, this was a not unwelcome development. However, as it continued well into the 1960s, and especially when the U.S. current account went into deficit in 1968, it was soon clear that a devaluation of the dollar was necessary.

Unfortunately, a mechanism for dealing with chronic payments imbalances and adjustments of the peg was never really finalized. As suggested earlier, Keynes had preferred arrangements that encouraged world growth. Consequently, his recommendations for reducing imbalances were aimed every bit as much (perhaps more so) at surplus countries as at deficit ones. He believed that the accumulation of surplus affected the world economy in the same way that savings reduced demand in a domestic economy.

The United States, as a likely creditor nation, balked at Keynes' plan. While White was sensitive to the problem that placing too much of the burden on the deficit country would be deflationary, it was widely believed by the U.S. contingent that the postwar economy was likely to be very inflationary (Bernstein 1989, p. 30; Walter 1991, pp. 155–156). The inability to arrive at a satisfactory compromise left them with no systematic means of addressing the issue (Walter 1991, pp. 154–156).

Thus, when "fundamental disequilibria" did occur, there was no automatic provision for dealing with them. And even though deficit countries were allowed considerable latitude to simply declare devaluations, in practice, the political implications of this kept them to a minimum (at least among the developed countries). Meanwhile, surplus countries were content to accumulate reserves.

To complicate matters, the United States was very reluctant to devalue given the status of the dollar as the international currency. Though an attempt was made to save Bretton Woods in 1971 (the Smithsonian Agreement), by 1973 the inability to agree on par rates led to its collapse. The reasons for its disintegration went beyond the inability to efficiently address payments imbalances.

The massive internationalization of capital that had been taking place since the late 1950s and early 1960s had placed tremendous pressure on the fixed-rate system. Keynes had already warned that capital controls would be necessary if central banks were to have the power to defend the parities set under Bretton Woods (Krause 1991, pp. 62–65). He recommended "not merely as a feature of the transition, but as a permanent arrangement . . . the right to control all capital movements" (Bryant 1987, pp. 61–62). As part of this policy, he submitted that all currency be converted through central banks.

Although market convertibility was substituted for official, Keynes' sentiment is reflected in the articles of agreement. Under Bretton Woods, pure capital flows could be, and were, controlled (Fraser 1987, pp. 19–28). In practice, each country put in place regulations intended to "balkanize" the various national capital markets (Krause 1991, p. 64).

However, as U.S. payments deficits caused dollars to accumulate in Europe, a combination of investors' desire to avoid the "balkanizing" controls and other considerations (such as U.S. limits on deposit interest and the growth of multinational industry and finance) led to the rise of the Eurodollar market.

From 1964 (the first year for which figures are available) to 1973, the Eurodollar market grew from the equivalent of $20 billion to $305 billion (Sarver 1988, pp. 6–7). The changing importance of the U.S. economy relative to Europe was already making the old par rates obsolete. The growing size of capital flows was now making actual and potential movements in exchange rates much larger, unpredictable, and uncontrollable.

With such capital available for speculation, apparent exchange rate problems quickly could become crises. By 1973, speculators had challenged and defeated every central bank, including the Federal Reserve (Moffitt 1983, pp. 71–92). The internationalization of capital had the potential to both cause and exacerbate fundamental disequilibria, and with no practical means of resolving these problems, Bretton Woods failed.

The failure of the World Bank to answer the challenge of world poverty, while less spectacular than the collapse of the Bretton Woods, has been far more tragic. The political ideology and economic approach of that institution have been so far removed from the realities of those struggling with underdevelopment that bank plans typically focus more on controlling inflation and introducing austerity plans than they do on addressing hunger and powerlessness (Danaher 1994).

The additional burden placed on so many in the third world by the debts created during the OPEC oil embargoes makes their future even more bleak. It does not appear that there is much about which to be encouraged regarding the policies that we may expect to see emerging from the World Bank in the near future.

Regarding international payments and exchange rates, immediately following the collapse of Bretton Woods, the stage was set for the continued growth and domination of the international capital market.

Today, the overwhelming majority of currency transactions are related to capital. As a consequence, policymakers are forced to consider the reaction of international financial markets to each and every policy move lest they be "punished" by capital outflows and currency depreciation or "rewarded" with inflows and appreciation.

Not only has this meant that the volume of capital led to excessive exchange rate volatility and chronic misalignment (Harvey 1995), but it also has created a deflationary bias in the system through the necessity of pleasing international investors with high interest rates and conservative economic policies (Davidson 1992–1993; Grabel 1993).

No true system has evolved to take the place of Bretton Woods. Instead, most developed country currencies float against one another (with one major exception, as explained below), whereas those of developing nations are pegged, most often to the dollar. For the developed countries, which continue to dominate trade and finance, the post–Bretton Woods era has been a managed float within which currency prices are set primarily by market forces, but central bank intervention still exists.

What triggers intervention depends on the economic and political objectives of the nation in question. One would think that this might create the potential for a great deal of conflict, but generally speaking, there have been more problems associated with market-initiated movements of the exchange rates, especially those associated with capital flows and speculation.

In fact, beginning with the Plaza Agreement in 1985, the central banks of France, Germany, Japan, Great Britain, and the United States have worked within broad guidelines to cooperate in introducing some stability into foreign exchange markets.

The major exception to market-determined rates among the developed countries has been the European Monetary System. It has operated as a mini-pegged system anchored to the Deutsche mark since 1979 and appeared to be moving toward a single-currency area until developments in 1992.

Just as in Bretton Woods, events made it clear that fundamental disequilibria existed and that changes in either macroeconomic policies or pegged rates were necessary.

Again similar to events in the early 1970s, agreement over what should be done was not easily had, and soon the massive force of speculation pushed policymakers to quickly choose which paths they would follow. By

1993, this had included extensive realignments and periods of floating and exchange rate bands so wide that they were "nearly tantamount to floating" (Henning 1994, p. 242). Whether this can be considered a success, only time will tell.

Ironically, the major issues that have plagued international monetary systems and agreements in the 50 years since the end of the World War II have been precisely those feared by Keynes in the early 1940s. In fixed-rate regimes, efficient means of realigning currencies remain elusive. Either the solutions tend to be deflationary, when they force deficit countries to contract their economies, or politically unpalatable, when they require currency devaluation.

Perhaps Keynes was correct when he saw the only viable means as placing the burden of adjustment on the surplus economy [a solution today urged by Paul Davidson (1992–1993)]. Meanwhile, capital flows have proven to be disruptive in both fixed- and flexible-rate systems, their "discipline" severely limiting policy choices in both circumstances. Success has been just as elusive regarding the World Bank and its work with less developed nations' economies.

Not surprisingly, the failures in both arenas have their roots in economic theory. Modern policymakers are convinced that market liberalization is the key to economic growth, so efforts to control capital flows directly or to plan or protect the economies of emerging states are unlikely to be forthcoming.

GLOSSARY

Annual report   The yearly year-end report of accounting companies send out to their shareholders.

Ask (offer) price   Ask is the market selling price, the price at which the market is prepared to sell a specified currency in a foreign exchange contract or cross-currency contract. At this price, the trader can buy the base currency. In the quotation, it is shown on the right side of the quotation, for instance, 1.4527–1.4532.

Base currency   This is the first currency in a currency pair, a currency against which the exchange rate is applied. Usually, it stands first in the codes of currency rates. It shows how much the base currency is worth as measured against the second currency. For instance, if the USD/CHF rate equals 1.6215, then one USD is worth CHF1.6215.

Bear   An investor who has taken a short position and believes prices will move lower.

Bear market   A market in which prices are declining.

Bid price   Bid is the market buying price, the price at which the market is prepared to buy a specified currency in a foreign exchange contract or cross-currency contract. At this price, the trader can sell foreign exchange. It is shown in the left side of the quotation, for example, 1.4527–1.4532.

Big figure quote   A currency rate without the last two digits. Examples: In a USD/JPY rate of 122.05/122.10, the big figure is 122. In a EUR/USD rate of 0.9325/0.9330, the big figure is 0.93.

Blank check   A shell company with no operating business that goes public with the interest of investing in another unspecified business.

Blind pool   Similar to blank check, except that an ordinary blind pool general lies specify what industry it plans to invest in.

Bull   One who expects the market to rise.

Bull market   A market in which prices are rising.

Business day   Any day on which commercial banks are open for business in the principal financial centers of the countries where currencies are traded.

Cash settled   The closing out of currency contracts with the exchange of cash based on the difference in the value of when the position was opened and the value of when it was closed rather than the delivery of currency.

Churning   When a broker trades an account excessively to generate commissions.

Cleared funds   Funds unencumbered and freely available and sent in to settle a trade.

Closed position   Exposures in foreign currencies that no longer exist. The process of closing a position is the selling or buying of a certain amount of currency to offset an equal amount of open positions. This will "square" the open position.

Commissions   The one-time fee charged by a broker to a customer after buying or selling a financial product, that is, stocks, commodities, or currencies. This process is also known as a *round turn*.

Confirmation   A notification sent by a dealer to a customer describing the terms of a trade.

Counter currency   The second listed currency in a currency pair.

Cross-currency pairs   A foreign exchange transaction in which one foreign currency is traded against a second foreign currency.

Cross-rate   An exchange rate between two non-U.S. currencies.

Currency symbols
    AUD   Australian dollar
    CAD   Canadian dollar
    EUR   Euro
    JPY   Japanese yen
    GBP   British pound
    CHF   Swiss franc

Currency trading   The act of exchanging the legal tender of one country for another.

Customer   The party that executes an agreement with a broker.

Currency pair   The two currencies that make up a foreign exchange rate, for example, USD/CHF.

Daily cutoff   The point in time for each business day selected by a broker to signify the end of the business day.

Day order   Any order that is placed for execution during only one trading session. If the order cannot be executed that day, it is automatically canceled.

Day trading   Establishing and liquidating the same position or positions within one day of trading, thus ending the day with no established position in the market.

Delivery   The tender and receipt of an actual commodity, financial instrument, or cash in settlement.

Delivery cutoff   The point in time that signifies the end of a trade date. The trade date of any contract entered into after the daily cutoff shall be the next business day.

Dollar value   The amount of lawful currency of the United States that at any moment in time would be generated by the conversion of the relevant foreign currency into U.S. dollars at the broker then-prevailing exchange rates for buying or selling such foreign currency.

Eligible foreign currencies   Those foreign currencies which the broker, in its sole discretion, may agree from time to time to buy from or sell to its customers.

Equity   The amount currently held in a customer's account calculated as if all the opened positions would be closed at the current market quotes. The account is composed of unrealized gains less unrealized losses and plus or minus storage.

Euro zone   The group of 12 countries that have combined their currencies into a single currency (euro). They still have separate sovereignties but also have a combined central bank (ECB) that handles economic policy issues for them as one group.

Fair market value   The price for a financial instrument that is determined in an open-market environment between a willing buyer and a willing seller.

Filled trade   A trade that is fully executed on behalf of a customer's account pursuant to an order. Once filled, an order cannot be canceled, amended, or waived by the customer.

Floating profit (loss)   Unrealized profit (loss) in an open position.

Free margin   Available funds in a client's account not currently being used to support existing trading positions, which can be used to open new positions.

Foreign currency   The legal tender issued by and acceptable for the payment of obligations under the laws of one or more countries.

Foreign exchange contract   A spot contract for the purchase or sale of a foreign currency.

Foreign exchange rate   The price relationships between two currencies that are freely determined by the forces of supply and demand.

Foreign exchange trading   Buying and selling foreign currencies.

Fundamental analysis   Analysis based on economic and political factors.

Gross basis   Open positions calculated without the benefit of any netting between long and short positions.

Good till Canceled (GTC) Order   A trade order placed for a specific amount of time to buy or sell a foreign currency.

Initial margin requirement or **opening margin requirement**   The minimum margin required to establish a new open position.

Leverage   The ratio of the amount used in a transaction to the required security deposit (margin).

Limit order   An order to buy or sell foreign currency or pairs of currencies at a specified price or exchange rate. A limit order to buy generally will be executed when the ask price equals or falls below the price or exchange rate specified in the limit order. A limit order to sell generally will be executed when the bid price equals or exceeds the price or exchange rate specified in the limit order. Customers should note, however, that market conditions often may prevent execution of an individual customer's limit order despite other dealing activity at that price level.

Liquidating order   An order to close out one or more open positions.

Long position   In foreign exchange trading, when the base currency in the pair is bought, the position is said to be long in that currency. It is understood that when the base currency in the pair is long, the second currency will be short.

Loss   Loss incurred as a result of a transaction.

Lot   A unit to measure the amount of a deal. The value of the deal always corresponds to an integer number of lots.

Margin   The amount of cash or other eligible collateral that the broker requires a customer to deposit or maintain in the customer's account in connection with the customer's trading activity.

Margin call   A demand for the deposit of additional margin as described in a customer agreement.

Market order   An order to buy or sell the identified currency or pairs of currencies at the current market price. An order to buy is executed at the ask price, and order to sell is executed at the bid price.

Market rate/quote   The current quote of a currency pair.

Market value   The dollar value, determined by the current foreign exchange rates, that a customer would receive if the position were liquidated for immediate delivery in the relevant market.

Mark to market   The process of recalculating the value of the open positions in a foreign currency trading account, assuming that all open positions were liquidated at current market rates.

Maturity   The date on which payment of a financial obligation is due.

Notice of withdrawal   A request by a customer to withdraw funds from the customer's account.

Offer (ask)   See *Ask (offer) price.*

One Cancels the Other (OCO) Order   Two orders that are linked. If one order is executed, the other is canceled.

Open position   Any deal that has not been offset by an equal and opposite deal.

Opening transaction   An order that, when executed, establishes a long position or short position or increases an existing position.

Order   Generally, an instruction by a customer (or customer's authorized agent) to a broker to attempt to execute a trade for the customer's account.

Overnight position   Trader's open long or short position that is not closed by the end of a trading day.

Pip/point   The smallest unit of price for any foreign currency [e.g., for USD/CHF one point (or pip) equals 0.0001 Swiss francs and for USD/JPY one point (or pip) equals 0.01 Japanese yen].

Position   An interest in the market, either long or short. Once an investor has bought or sold to enter the market, he or she has taken a position.

Posted margin   That part of the margin balance that is posted to the broker in support of the customer's open position and unrealized losses.

Profit/Loss (P/L) or **gain/loss**   The actual gain or loss in U.S. dollars resulting from trading activities on closed positions, plus the theoretical gain or loss on open positions that have been marked to market.

Quote   A simultaneous bid and offer in a currency pair.

Rally   An upward movement of prices after a decline. The opposite of a reaction.

Range   The high and low prices or high and low bids and offers recorded during a specified time.

Reaction   A decline in prices after an advance. The opposite of a rally.

Realized gain/loss   The actual gain or loss resulting from closing an open position.

Resistance   A significant price level which has been tested and found to act as a strong price ceiling.

Rollovers   The process of extending an existing market position through one or more spot settlements.

Scalp   Scalping normally involves establishing and liquidating a position quickly, usually within the same day, same hour, or even within a few minutes. A day trader is a scalper.

Short margin   A client's account condition when equity becomes smaller than the amount required to keep the positions open.

Short position   Selling a currency in which you have no position in anticipation of it falling in value. At that point you will be able to "cover" your short by buying back the currency at a lower price. (If physical delivery of the currency is involved, the short seller will need to borrow the currency in order to make the delivery to the buyer.) In foreign exchange, when the base currency in the pair is sold, the position is said to be short in that currency. It is understood that when the base currency in the pair is short, the second currency will be long.

Spot contract   A contract where settlement is in two business days.

Spot rate   The rate of exchange between two foreign currencies for spot value (normally settlement in two business days), generally quoted either in U.S. terms (price of one unit of foreign currency expressed in U.S. dollars and cents) or in European terms (price of one U.S. dollar expressed in units and decimals of the foreign currency).

Spread   The difference between the ask (offer) and bid prices in a market quote. The spread is the reason why a newly opened position's mark to market, or valuation, likely will be negative. If a trader buys a particular currency, he or she will pay the ask (offer) price, but the current mark to market will be based on what the marketplace is presently paying for this currency. That price would be found on the bid side of the market quote, 5 pips lower than where the trader just bought the currency.

Stop/loss order An order to buy or sell at a specified foreign exchange rate away from the current market for the purpose of liquidating an open position during market conditions in which the open position has declined in value. Execution of such an order can occur at rates below (or above) the specified foreign exchange rate.

Storage The charge or recompense associated with a rollover.

Support A significant price level which has been tested and found to act as a strong price floor.

Technical analysis Analysis of market price action. Technical analysis studies historical price changes with the aim to forecast future price movements. By studying price charts and a host of supporting technical indicators, traders in effect let the market tell them which way it is most likely to trend. The whole purpose of charting the price action of a market is to identify trends in the early stages of their development and then trade in the direction of those trends. One of the two types of analysis used to analyze the currency market.

Tick Refers to a change in price, either up or down. Also called one pip on the FOREX.

Trade date With respect to any contract, the date on which the contract is entered into between the broker and customer, except in the case of any contract entered into after the daily cutoff following but before the next relevant business day, in which case the trade date shall be the next following business day.

Trend The general direction of the market.

Unrealized gain/loss The theoretical gain or loss on open positions valued at current market rates, as determined by the broker in its sole discretion. Unrealized gains/losses become profits/losses when the position is closed.

Used margin The amount in a client's account required to support all the current positions.

Value date With respect to any contract, the applicable settlement date specified in the confirmation that relates to the particular contract. A value date must fall on a business day in the countries of the traded currencies.

Volume The number of transactions made during a specified period of time.

BIBLIOGRAPHY

Bank of America. "2001 Annual Report." Bank of America May 01, 2002. <http://s1.mobular.net/ccbn/7/27/29/>

Elliott, R. N. *Nature's Law – The Secret of the Universe*. Commodity Traders Club, Phoenix, AZ., 1995.

Knox, Noelle. "N.Y. Attorney General Widens Investigation." *USA Today* Apr 11, 2002: B.01

Vickers, Marcia and Mike France, Emily Thornton, David Henry, and Heather Timmons "How Corrupt Is It?" *BusinessWeek* May 13 2002: 36.

Luca, Cornelius. *Technical Analysis Application in the Global Currency Market.-2nd ed*. New York Institute of Finance, New York, NY, 2000.

Luca, Cornelius. *Trading in the Global Currency Makret.-2nd ed*. New York Institute of Finance, New York, NY, 2000.

Plocek, Joseph E. *Economic Indicators*. New York Institute of Finance, New York, NY, 1991.

Shimizu, Seiki. *The Japanese Chart of Charts*. Tokyo Futures Trading Publishing Company, Tokyo, Japan, 1996.

Waggoner, John and Thomas Fogarty. "Scandals Shred Investors' Faith" *USA Today* May 2, 2002: A.01

CHARTS, FIGURES AND CREDITS

eSignal, 3955 Point Eden Way, Hayward, CA 94545. <http://www.esignal.com>

4X Made Easy/GlobalTec Solutions, 5010 Addison Circle, Addison TX 75001.

Forex Capital Markets FXCM, Financial Square 32 Old Slip 10th Floor, New York, NY 10005.

Cover photo by Peter Burg. Burg Photographix <http://www.burgphoto.com>

Index

About the Author

James Dicks, the founder of 4x Made Easy™, is the president and CEO of Premiere*fx*, LLC. He is an author, teacher and CEO of a growing network of international companies focused on helping investors from all walks of life learn how to diversify their portfolios and practice good money management. Mr. Dicks has inspired and founded the fastest-selling financial software for trading the FOREX, and is the leading trainer in the world for international currency trading and investing. Mr. Dicks has held numerous professional licenses in the securities field starting in early 1991, and occupies investment advisor or capital development positions for growing entities.

Trading for more than 13 years, James has witnessed markets of all types and started trading the FOREX as a way to better diversify his portfolio, the same way big banks and Fortune 1000 companies do. With a simple message of diversification and good money management, James shares with you the largest financial market in the world.

James is a dynamic trainer and motivator, speaking on nationally syndicated radio shows and appearing nationally before thousands of people educating them on personal finance, real estate, and investing. He is a current member of the Marine Corps League, and is proud to have served in the United States Marine Corps.